# Go Ahead...Proof It!

K.D. SULLIVAN

BARRON'S

## Dedication

To my son John, who I am so very proud of, and
who is very proud of me.

All inquiries should be addressed to:
Barron's Educational Series, Inc.
250 Wireless Boulevard
Hauppauge, New York 11788

Library of Congress Catalog Card No.: 96-7454

International Standard Book No.: 0-8120-9744-0

**Library of Congress Cataloging-in-Publication Data**
Sullivan, K.D.
        Go ahead . . . proof it! / K.D. Sullivan.
            p.    cm.
        Includes bibliographical references and index.
        ISBN 0-8120-9744-0
        1. Proofreading.  I. Title.
    Z254.S87    1996
    686.2′255—dc20                                          96-7454
                                                                CIP

PRINTED IN THE UNITED STATES OF AMERICA
987654321

# Table of Contents

Introduction    **1**

Chapter 1   **Before You Know the Inside Scoop**    **7**

     PDU Campus News    8

     Proofreader's Marks Plus Examples    10

Chapter 2   **What First?**    **13**

     Before You Begin    16

     Stage 1: The First Readthrough    18

     Style Sheets    18

     Sample Document Style Sheet    22

     Cross-References    31

Chapter 3   **The Basics Made More Basic**    **33**

     Spelling    33

     Grammar    36

     Punctuation    40

## Chapter 4 What Comes Next? 45

Stage 2: Chapter Number and
Chapter Title 48

Stage 3: Headings 49

Stage 4: Numbered Lists and
Bulleted Lists 50

Stage 5: Captions 51

Stage 6: Running Heads and Folios 54

Stage 7: Table of Contents 55

Stage 8: A Final Look 55

Finals Check 56

## Chapter 5 Special Circumstances 59

Proofreading for a Publisher 59

Advertising Copy 63

Retail Catalogs 64

## Chapter 6 After You're Filled In 67

Corrected Versions of Fiction,
Press Release, and Minutes
Proofreading Exercises 69

PDU Campus News 71

PDU Campus News Corrected
Version Queries 75

# Appendix A

     Words Often Misspelled     77

     Words Often Confused     78

# Appendix B     81

     Glossary of Publishing-Related Terms     81

# Recommended References     88

# Index     89

# Introduction

Believe it or not, you already know how to proofread. After all, isn't proofreading just reading carefully? Then why read this book? Because it's full of insider tips that will train you to proofread like a pro.

You may ask, "With computer spell check and grammar check, is there anything left for a proofreader to check?" The answer is a resounding yes! First, not everyone works on a computer. Second, and much more important, as helpful as computer tools are, there are still no replacements for the human mind and eye.

*Go Ahead...Proof It!* is not a highly technical book about proofreading. While this book covers some of the biggest grammar and punctuation problem areas, it does not cover punctuation or capitalization rules in depth, or detail all the nuances of grammar and word usage. There are already many well-known references on those subjects. Some of these books are included in the recommended references section at the end of the book. *Go Ahead...Proof It!* illustrates the major steps that will benefit anyone proofreading a simple letter, a two-page brochure, or a whole book who wants to turn out a quality product.

When you *proofread*, you are making sure a final written product lives up to its author's intentions, whether that product is a book manuscript, the minutes from last week's staff meeting, your roommate's term paper, your grandmother's letter to the editor of a local newspaper, or a press release you've drafted announcing your new business. In other words, when wearing the proofreader's hat, as a professional or an amateur, it is up to you to catch any errors the writer (your boss, client, friend, even yourself) might have missed. It is important to note that proofreading does not entail editing or rewriting; rather it encompasses smoothing out a product's rough edges by checking and correcting any mistakes.

Sound like a lot of responsibility? It is. And if you are the sole author, editor, and word processor—as is often the case in desktop publishing—it is especially challenging!

## FROM BLANK PAGE TO BOUND COPY: TRADITIONAL PUBLISHING

Any written project must undergo a series of stages before it is finalized and disseminated to its intended audience (teacher, client, general public). Traditional book publishers have, over the years, developed an effective path written material must travel down before it is set in stone and shipped off to your local bookstore. A very simplified version of these steps follows:

1. The **author** writes the material, often onto a disk. Whether it is 1 page or 1,000 pages, this is called the *manuscript.*

2. The manuscript is given to an **editor** (sometimes called a developmental or content editor). The editor may suggest a style or format of writing. The editor may rewrite or restructure sentences, paragraphs, or even chapters to help communicate the material in the required format or tone, or with the appropriate marketing focus.

3. Once the author and editor have made their changes, a fresh copy of the manuscript is printed out and goes to the **copy editor**. Although there are different levels of copy-editing, the copy editor's job is to correct errors in spelling, grammar, consistency, design, and style, while maintaining the author's style of writing. The copy editor

also *queries* (questions) any areas of concern along the way. In addition, the copy editor prepares a *style sheet* (a list of words, numbers, phrases, and designs that could be handled in more than one way, that are the style choices to be followed for a specific project).

4. After the book design is determined, the copyedited manuscript goes to a **typesetter, word processor**, or **desktop person** to incorporate all this information and print out a set of *page proofs* (sometimes just called a set of pages).

5. The page proofs go to the **proofreader**, whose job it is to check that the typeset copy exactly matches the copyedited manuscript. The proofreader marks errors and queries areas in which she or he feels there is an editorial error.

Authors, editors, and proofreaders who work for publishers may feel that some of the material presented in this book as the job of the proofreader is actually the responsibility of the authors and editors. Traditionally, their description of a proofreader's job is only to *verify* that typeset material appears as requested by the authors and editors. But being aware of the steps that precede the proofreading stage, plus taking the time and having the expertise to verify and correct more than just spelling and punctuation, makes you a better proofreader, and a much more valuable asset—to yourself and your clients!

This brings us to our first insider tip.

---

**INSIDER TIP**

In addition to catching spelling, grammar, and punctuation errors, what turns a good proofreading job into an excellent one is the element of *consistency*. For example, if you hyphenate "first-time reader" on page 1 of your document, you shouldn't spell "first time reader" without a hyphen later.

---

## PROOFREADING FOR CLIENTS OTHER THAN PUBLISHERS

If you are doing all the previously listed steps yourself, chances are you will combine some of them. You may be editing as you are typesetting.

If you proofread for clients other than publishers, some of these steps get shortcut, or skipped altogether. Also, the lines between copyediting and proofreading responsibilities become more blurred. For example, depending on the client and the project, you may be asked to do an *editorial proofread*, combining the tasks of proofreading and light copyediting.

In my fifteen years of experience as a proofreader, I've worked on projects ranging from 1-page advertising copy to 1,500-page computer books, from marketing plans to murder mysteries. Even though each project is unique, certain steps apply to them all. So, now let's use the benefits of *my* experience to take *your* skills to a higher level.

One of the most important lessons to learn about proofreading is

> *You achieve an accurate and consistent finished product by proofreading in stages.*

And that is what *Go Ahead...Proof It!* shows. It gives a complete explanation of how this proofreading process contributes to consistency and how you can use it to turn out high-quality documents.

To get you involved right away, Chapter 1 presents a sample college newsletter for you to proofread. This exercise will show you what you know about proofreading and what mistakes you are able to catch at this time. The four chapters that follow the newsletter describe the Eight Stages of Proofreading and how they can be applied to any project, no matter how simple or complex. Also included in this chapter is a list of proofreader's marks, which is much more than just a list. It also contains examples of how to use the marks: what would be marked in the text, what would be marked in the margin, and how the change should appear after it has been corrected.

Chapters 2 and 3 concentrate on how to make Stage 1 of proofreading most productive. They outline some simple ways to sharpen the skills you already have and point out some basic recurring problems. They also cover proofreader's marks and discuss in detail a *style sheet* (another insider tip). The first stage, however, is only the beginning.

Chapter 4 discusses what happens next. It covers the other stages of proofreading, which help *refine* your document. Although you may find some familiar information here, you will probably find some information you may never have considered before.

Chapter 5 addresses a few, more complex, specialized cases. Some projects, such as retail catalogs, computer books, advertising copy, and works of fiction, can call for specific proofreading rules or techniques. Chapter 5 gives you that special edge so you can handle these projects with confidence.

Chapter 6 provides three short proofreading exercises, and another copy of the newsletter you proofread at the beginning of the book. Try proofreading it again and compare your corrections with those you marked before. You may be pleasantly surprised at how many more mistakes you now find. Finally, the newsletter is presented once more—this time with all the corrections marked. Did you catch all these?

For easy reference, Appendix A lists words often misspelled and words often confused, and Appendix B is a glossary of publishing-related terms.

The recommended references section lists some books that cover individual subjects thoroughly. If you need to find an item quickly, the detailed index will assist you.

Not everything in this book applies to every project, but it is a good idea to read everything, because it will increase your awareness of what to look for. This book should help you do a more professional job, answer any questions you may have, and answer questions you didn't even know you had.

# Chapter 1

## Before You Know the Inside Scoop

The sample newsletter that follows is peppered with mistakes for you to find. Some are obvious and some aren't. Mark what you find using the proofreading marks on pages 10 and 11, or any marks you like, as long as they are clear to you. If you are unsure if a specific correction should be made, make a note of the question for yourself. You can put the note on a sticky tag next to the text in question or you can put numbers next to the text you are unsure about, and then their corresponding questions on a separate piece of paper.

This will be your *before* picture. The same newsletter appears in Chapter 6 for you to proofread again after you have completed reading this book. That will be your *after* picture.

# PDU CAMPUS NEWS

**VOLUME 10, NUMBER 8**                    **FALL ISSUE**

## The Tide is Turning—Gray

*By Ann Longknife*

I entered my new literture class expecting the usual eager (and not so eager) young students who would grow wise from my relayed wisdom. I was surprised, however, to see an old lady sitting in the front row. She was Betty, 86 years old, in school becuase she wanted to know more about literture. Betty is only one of the older students now coming to college. They are changing the classroom, generaly for the better.

In the past, the older student was an anomoly in the community college classroom, but that has changed. Re-entry women return to learn new skills. Some people who have lost their jobs return for retraining. And many return to enhance their lives now that they are established and their children are grown.

These students weren't considered valuble by the State of California. A few years ago Governor Wilson decreed, and the legislature agreed, to raise fees, from $13 a credit hour to $50, for those students who already have a degree. Enrollment dropped and the schools collected neither the $13 nor the $50. Last year the law was rescinded— now the older students are back.

There varied experiences give a new perspective to class discussions so the younger students learn about many different views rather than just their own or the instructors. In turn, the older students learn how young people think which gives them better rapport with their own children and, often, their colleagues at work.

The instructor, however, needs to make this sharing a positive experience. I've found some ways to do this. I call every one by their first name, which makes the students feel they are equals. Sometimes, older students monopolize the conversations. This can be deadly, so I call on people by name. That way everyone gets to contribute. When I share papers with the class, I make sure I acheive a balance between those of older students and younger. Most importantly, I treat the answers of all the students with respect. If I favored one group, the class would not work.

The baby boomers, as we've been told repeatedly, are older—and perhaps wiser, for they are coming back to learn what they missed earlier. They can be a source of income for the community college, but, more importanly, they can promote a lively, energetic environment where all students, regardless of age, can get a better education.

## By my Own Rules: Confessions of a freelance writer

*By Michelle Goodman*

Self-employed, innovator, entreprenuer, consultant, freelancer, independent contractor, jill-of-all-trades, small business owner, armchair professional, artist, creative type, dreamer. Chances are you know somebody you'd classify as one of these. Between my accountant and my family, I've personally been called as everything from "1099 worker" to "slacker".

As a self-employed writer, I'm often regarded as rule-breaking rebel, a curiosity in a world of synchronized commuting and coffee breaks. And justifiably so. Take my obscure work habits, for instance: While you're rushing off to the office at 8:15 a.m. in your dry-cleaned suit, I'm propped up

*Continued on page 3*

1

Continued from page 2
in bed, wearing a ratty old bathrobe, pecking away at my laptop computer. When Letterman's over and you turn off the light to sleep, I'm nursing a pot of coffee, trying to wring a few more productive hours out of the day. Tomorrow during your 3 o' clock meeting I might be napping in the park, hiking along the beach, or watching Oprah.

When you work for yourself, you're not just breaking the pre-existing rules of the 9-to-5 workforce, you're writing your own comandments of employment, then rewriting them as you go. I can e-mail press releases and advertising copy I write to a handful of clients I'll probably never even meet face to face, thanks to my faithful computer modem. And sometimes I'll work 15-hour days for a straight week, then send out my invoice and kick back and relax the following week.

People always ask me how I can work in my house, alone all day long, tempted by all the procrastination-inducing distractions of home (fridge, TV, phone, newspaper). Then they want to know what on Earth could have compelled me to give up the steady paycheck and benefits package that I may or may nod be blessed with were I a "regular" company employee. For me the how and why of my choice to work this way is one and the same: Being master of my own destiny—free to stay up late and sleep in, saved from the stress and exhaustion of the dreaded 5-day-a-week commute, free to spend more time doing what I want to do—is far more rewarding than the so-called advantages of any "real" job.

## A Profile of ESL Students At PDU

As social, economic, and political circumstances create the conditions for immigration to the U.S., a large number of speakers of other languages are striving to become literate in English. In recent years, PDU has experienced considerable growth in the number of language minority students seeking to become literate in English.

Figure 1 depicts students' ESL proficiency in terms of their current course level (i.e., 841, 842,

843 and 844): 39.7% of student are enrolled in 844-level coursework; 29.6% in 843-level; 14.7% in 842-level, and 15.1% in 841-level.

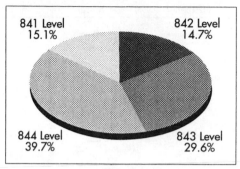

**Figure 1**
Current ESL Proficiency Level

Figure 2 shows that between approximately one-quarter to one third of students expressed an interest in taking ESL courses during each of the four following times:

1. 7:00 am–8:00 am M–F (29.3%)

2. Saturday mornings (26.8%)

3 5:00 pm–6:00 pm M–F (20.4%)

An additional 25.6% indicated "other times; these included Sunday mornings, Sunday evenings, Saturday evenings, and 6:00am M-F courses.

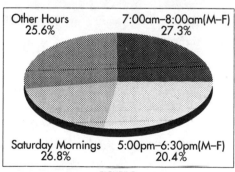

**FIGURE 2**
Interest in alternative days for ESL classes

2

## PROOFREADER'S MARKS PLUS EXAMPLES

| Explanation (Alphabetically) | Marked In Margin* | Marked In Text | After Correction |
| --- | --- | --- | --- |
| Align | align | 10<br>  20<br>30 | 10<br>20<br>30 |
| Boldface | bf | Warning! | **Warning!** |
| Capitalize | cap | snap | Snap |
| Close up | cu | Crackl e | Crackle |
| Delete | ℰ or ℰ | Popp | Pop |
| Delete and close up | ℰ | nonↄprofit | nonprofit |
| Equal spacing | eq #ing | Exercise every day. | Exercise every day. |
| Insert: | | | |
| Apostrophe | ⌄ | Its yours. | It's yours. |
| Colon | ⌄ | Contains two red and blue. | Contains two: red and blue. |
| Comma | ⌄ | guitar, drums and keyboard | guitar, drums, and keyboard |
| Em dash | m | Create the moment then hold it. | Create the moment—then hold it. |
| En dash | N | 1920 1930 | 1920–1930 |
| Hyphen | = | fast moving car | fast-moving car |
| Letter | n | ed | end |
| -closed up on left | ↄ s | end | ends |
| -closed up on right | m ↄ | end | mend |
| Parentheses | ( / ) ** | 3 sizes a, b, c | 3 sizes (a, b, c) |

\*With the exception of the mark for a period, instructions that should not be set in print—like rebreak, stet, ital, and so on—are circled; words, letters, and symbols that should be set, are not circled.

\*\*Note diagonal lines to indicate more than one change on one line.

## PROOFREADER'S MARKS PLUS EXAMPLES
### (continued)

| Explanation (Alphabetically) | Marked In Margin* | Marked In Text | After Correction |
|---|---|---|---|
| Insert: (cont.) | | | |
| Period | | Let's eat‸ | Let's eat. |
| Question mark | | Why stop‸ | Why stop? |
| Quotation marks | ** | He wrote,‸I remember my mother's words,‸Never fear to dream.‸ | He wrote, "I remember my mother's words, 'Never fear to dream.'" |
| Semicolon | | Stop and look‸ then listen. | Stop and look; then listen. |
| Space | # | a‸lot | a lot |
| Word | come | Please‸here. | Please come here. |
| Italicize | ital | the Chronicle | the *Chronicle* |
| Lowercase | lc | Keep ⁄rying. | Keep trying. |
| Move: Up | ⌐ | Stand⌐up⌐ | Stand up |
| Down | ⌐ | Sit⌐down⌐ | Sit down |
| Left | ⊏ | Fight, ⊏ Fight, | Fight, Fight, |
| Right | ⊐ | ⊐Fight | Fight |
| Rebreak | rebreak | pos‐ ible | pos‐ sible |
| Small caps | sc | 8:00 p.m. | 8:00 P.M. |
| Spell out | sp | Knock③times. | Knock three times. |
| Stet (keep original text) | stet | Read very carefully. | Read very carefully. |
| Transpose | tr | ca⁀ual | casual |
| Wrong size | ws | 9–14–7⑤ | 9–14–75 |

*With the exception of the mark for a period, instructions that should not be set in print—like rebreak, stet, ital, and so on—are circled; words, letters, and symbols that should be set, are not circled.

**Note diagonal lines to indicate more than one change on one line.

# Chapter 2

## What First?

Nobody is perfect, not even proofreaders (although most of us might argue this point). If you have ever worked in an office, you know how many times a project can change hands (and pens or computer keyboards) and you have no doubt seen how easy it is for errors to creep into documents. Here is an example of what can happen.

A boss (the author) prepares a memo (the manuscript):

Effective June 1, flex-time with be offered to all

full-time and part-time employees. The hours

may be arranged with your supervisor so that all

workstations will be covered and efficency will not

be effected. We will do our best to accomodate

your schedule requests.

Then it goes to one or two company department heads (the editors) who put in their two cents' worth:

Effective June 1, flex-time with be offered to all

full-time and part-time employees. The hours

*must*
~~may~~ be arranged with your supervisor so that all

*fully staffed*
workstations will be ~~covered~~ and efficency will not

be effected. We will do our best to accomodate

your schedule requests.

Next it goes to an executive assistant (the copy editor) to make sure the mechanics (grammar, spelling, punctuation) of the memo are correct:

Effective June 1, flex-time *will* ~~with~~ be offered to all

full-time and part-time employees. The hours

*must*
~~may~~ be arranged with your supervisor so that all

*fully staffed* *i*
workstations will be ~~covered~~ and efficency will not

*a* *m*
be effected. We will do our best to accomodate

your schedule requests.

The edited memo needs to be typed or word processed. Then this copy (the page proof) needs to be proofread against the manuscript. Once the errors are marked to be changed, it goes back to word processing to make the corrections. That's it, right? Not quite. Deciding not to proofread again, since only a few corrections were made, can have dire consequences:

Effective June 1, flextime will be offered to all full-time and part-time employees. The hours must be arranged with your supervisor so that all worksta-tions will be fully stuffed and efficiency will not be affected. We will do our best to accommodate your schedule requests.

Anytime corrections are made, a document should be reproofread. If time permits, the whole document should be reproofed. If time is short, see the section "Finals Check" in Chapter 4 for some shortcuts on proofreading already proofed material. The more people involved in the creation of written material, the more room for potential mistakes. That is why people depend on proofreaders.

Some people are also lax about checking their work because they have come to rely on computers to catch their mistakes. Although computers do catch many typographical errors (*typos*), they cannot distinguish grammatically between **now** and **not**. Both are spelled correctly; but put them in a sentence incorrectly and a computer can't tell the difference.

---

**INSIDER TIP**

If you are working online, it is a good idea to print out what you need to proofread. For most people, it is more effective to proof a paper version (often called the *hard copy*) than to proofread directly on the screen.

---

Whether you are proofreading for an employer or a relative, do not hesitate to *query* (another word for question) something that does not make sense, or to suggest minor changes that you think would improve the material. As long as you do it in a polite and professional manner, most people will appreciate your input. After all, everyone is working toward the same goal—an accurate, quality product.

## BEFORE YOU BEGIN

As I said in the Introduction, the most effective way to proofread is in *stages*. Even letters and school papers (teachers would say especially school papers) benefit from more than one read, since it is sometimes difficult to look for everything at one time.

---

**INSIDER TIP**

When proofreading, try to always sit in a comfortable chair that supports your back and legs. Make sure you have proper lighting (daylight and halogen light are two excellent choices). It's best to set your copy at an upward angle with the text as close to eye level as possible. Your body will appreciate the care you're giving it.

---

### Comparison Proofreading Versus Straight Read

Most proofreading projects fall into two categories: comparison proofreading and straight read.

*Comparison proofreading* entails comparing a final version (in book publishing it is usually called a *page proof*) against an edited version (usually called the *manuscript* in publishing). Allow yourself enough room to set the stack of manuscript pages and the stack of page proofs next to each other. Then as you complete each page, place them text down to the right and left of your original stacks.

Here you are checking to see that the final version matches exactly what is in the original version, including any handwritten changes made by the author, or any number of editors. Even when checking your own work, comparison proofing is always best if you have the time—and essential if it is your first time proofreading the material. Say, for example, you have a handwritten rough draft of your résumé and your final typed copy, or even two typed copies. Compare these two versions word for word to make sure none of your great ideas got "lost in the translation" (as in the memo example on pages 13–15).

---

**INSIDER TIP**

**Whenever possible, ask someone else to look over your work after you have proofed it. Reading the same material over and over may blind you to obvious errors. A fresh perspective never hurts.**

---

When proofreading for a client, there are times you may be asked to just do a *straight read*, which means reading only one version, without comparing it against a manuscript. Sometimes this is because the document is at an early stage and the client wants your input before paying for typesetting. Sometimes the client is confident the typesetter has set everything correctly.

## Marking the Page Proofs

Standard practice for comparison proofreading is to mark changes both in the text and in the margin, which serves two purposes. First, the changes you are requesting are less likely to be overlooked. Second, there is more room in the margins to write out the changes you are making, which makes it easier for the person implementing your changes to see what you are asking for. Always be considerate of the person performing the next phase of the job—yourself included. (Note that when authors and editors make changes to a manuscript, they mark the changes in the text only.) Two other sources containing a complete list of proofreaders' marks are *Webster's Collegiate Dictionary*, under (surprise!) proofreader's marks, and *The Chicago Manual of Style*.

Although it is best to become fluent in these marks—they are the universal language of publishing—it is not crucial. What *is* crucial is marking your corrections clearly, so there is no question about the changes you are making.

One caution here: When proofreading for someone else, make sure you and your clients are "on the same page" about what they want. Is this a comparison or straight read? Should you use standard proofreading marks or not? Do they want queries on Post-its or written right on the pages? Also, what level of proofreading do they expect: "just" a check for spelling, grammar, punctuation, sense, and consistency? Do they simply want you to query any awkward wording, or do they want you to suggest ways to reword the material? Although the latter is not usually the proofreader's responsibility, many people appreciate the input from an experienced proofreader—that's you!

## STAGE 1: THE FIRST READTHROUGH

The first stage is called the *first readthrough*. Here you are looking for errors in spelling, grammar, punctuation, and consistency, and to see if what you are reading makes sense. It helps if when you read you become the audience. Ask yourself: Are the ideas presented clearly and concisely? Does the material make sense?

## STYLE SHEETS

Simply put, a style sheet is a list of all words, numbers, phrases, and *style choices* (items that could be handled in more than one way, so these are the choices you are to follow) that will be used to ensure consistency in a project. A style sheet can be formal or informal, handwritten or typed, short or long. It should be comprehensive enough to answer the questions of anyone, at any stage

---

**INSIDER TIP**

**If you have to read a sentence or phrase more than once because it doesn't make sense, stop! That sentence or phrase needs attention. But before you change or query it, read the sentence or phrase out loud. Reading out loud slows you down and allows you to focus on each nuance of the sentence, making it easier to identify where the problem lies.**

---

of the project. Traditionally, the style sheet is prepared by the copy editor, if there is one on the project.

Often there are elements in a project that need to follow strict rules; a style sheet provides a way to keep track of these rules. The word **by-product**, for example, should be hyphenated, according to *Webster's Collegiate Dictionary*. However, people tend to use **byproduct** (one word) or **by product** (two words, no hyphen). With **by-product** on the style sheet, you know from the beginning of the project that this is a word you need to watch for, to be sure it is spelled correctly.

You will also find there are many issues regarding punctuation, spelling, capitalization, hyphenation, fonts, and so on that are a matter of preference—these are style choices. Anytime there might be more than one way to handle an issue, this should appear on the style sheet. The style sheet is an invaluable tool for the proofreader.

For example, you may see the word **prohibition** in your text, and the first time you encounter it, it is all lowercase. The next time, it is **Prohibition**, with the first letter capitalized (called *initially capped* or *icapped* ). Once the decision is made on how it should appear—all lowercase, for example—this should be included on the style sheet. This way everyone working on the project will know how this word should appear by looking at the style sheet.

Even if you are the only one working on the project, sometimes it is tough to remember when you see **Prohibition** on one page, whether it was lowercase or initially capped when it appeared earlier. Or perhaps several people have contributed written material to a project. One person may always lowercase this word and another always initially cap it. With **prohibition** on the style sheet, there is no confusion: On this job, it should always appear lowercase. On other jobs, it may appear both ways depending on the context in which it is used.

Sometimes industry standards dictate a style choice. For example, in *Webster's Collegiate Dictionary* the word **nonprofit** has no hyphen. Yet the standard usage among many nonprofit organizations is **non-profit** (hyphenated). If the decision is to spell it **non-profit** (hyphenated), that should be recorded on the style sheet. That way any well-meaning people who work on the project later won't take the hyphen out, thinking they are helping. They will be able to see from the style sheet that the hyphen is correct.

It is important that as many style decisions as possible are made *before* beginning to write, edit, or proofread a project. That way everyone involved with the project starts out working with the same guidelines.

As mentioned earlier, when a project is professionally edited, the copy editor will usually prepare a style sheet, but that is not always the case. If you do not receive a style sheet with your proofreading job, it is important to make up your own.

If you are working on a short project, you might want to just jot down a few general notes on a sheet of paper, as shown in this example for a fictional advertising agency:

### Interoffice Memo
### for Pacific Advertising Agency

a.m.
flextime
full-time (adj., n.)
job-sharing
policymaker

If it is a long work, such as a thesis or book, you want a more extensive style sheet. A discussion of the different kinds of style sheets follows.

## Document Style Sheet

Style choices may vary from document to document. The Sample Document Style Sheet on pages 22–25 is in a format that has been used for years. It is a fairly extensive style sheet that gives you several examples of what might appear on one. Most items on this style sheet could be handled in more than one way. Not all the style choices on the sample are necessarily standards to follow; they are style *choices*. A majority of companies and publishers, however, have adopted the conventions on this Sample Document Style Sheet. Since it is not possible to cover every questionable situation in this book, this style sheet suggests some things that you might not think required a decision.

## SAMPLE DOCUMENT STYLE SHEET

Author _____ Title _____

If you need more space for a given category, use adjacent unneeded space, but change headings so that they will be applicable.

| Numbers and Dates | Abbreviations |
|---|---|
| 1990s (not 1990's)<br>spell out one to ten;<br>numerals for 11 and up<br>1:00 PM<br>phone numbers: 415-555-1212<br>decimals: 0.05 (not .05)<br>two-year-old<br>2 years' experience<br>8 ½-by-11-inch paper<br>pp. 10 to 15 | U.S. (as adjective; spell out as noun)<br>J. L. Dyson (space between name initials)<br>G.N.P. |

| Punctuation | Headings |
|---|---|
| italicize punctuation following italicized text<br>don't boldface punctuation following boldface text<br>use series comma (A, B, and C)<br>in lists: If one entry is a complete sentence or contains a complete sentence, each entry takes an ending period; otherwise no ending periods. | capitalize articles, prepositions, etc. of 5 or more letters; lowercase less than 5:<br>Look for Sections About Style Sheets<br>Initially cap both parts of Compound words:<br>High-Density Disks<br>Non-Yellowing Paper |

## SAMPLE DOCUMENT STYLE SHEET

| Indicate the following and other abbreviations when appropriate:<br><br>(n) noun<br>(v) verb<br>(a) adjective<br>(adv) adverb<br>(W) per *Webster's Collegiate Dictionary* | A<br><br>acknowledgment<br>adviser<br>  (not advisor)<br>appendixes<br>awhile (but:<br>  for a while) | B<br><br>back up (v) (W)<br>backup (n,a) (W)<br>the Bay Area<br>buses<br>by-products<br>  (W) | C<br><br>canceling<br>  (one "l")<br>catalog<br>check mark<br>check-out time<br>coworker (W) |
|---|---|---|---|
| D<br><br>database<br>descendant<br>disk (not disc) | E<br>Earth (as planet)<br>earth, the<br>equal sign<br>  (not equals<br>    sign)<br>every day<br>everyday (a) (W) | F<br>federal law<br>file name<br>follow up (v) (W)<br>followup (a) (W) | G<br><br>gray (not grey)<br>good-bye |
| H<br>health care (n)<br>health-care (a)<br>high-quality (a)<br>highest quality (a) | I–J–K<br>judgment | L<br>left-hand (a) (W)<br>life force (W)<br>lifestyle  (W)<br>log on (v)<br>logon (n,a)<br>lowercase (W) | M<br>movable<br>multiuser |

## SAMPLE DOCUMENT STYLE SHEET

| N | O | P–Q | Permissions Required |
|---|---|---|---|
| nonˉ<br>(always closed)<br>(like non drip, nonskid) | okay<br>online (n)<br>on-line (a,adv) (W)<br>onscreen (n)<br>on-screen (a,adv) (W) | pick up (v) (W)<br>pickup (n,a) (W)<br>Post-it ™ | Use this column to list numbers of pages containing non-original matter for which permissions may be required. |
| R<br>real time (n)<br>real-time (a)<br>recreate<br>re-create (create again) (W)<br>right-hand (a) (W)<br>rightmost (W) | S<br>an SMI event<br>southern California<br>start up (v) (W)<br>startup (n,a) (W)<br>Styrofoam (W) | T<br>traveled (one "l")<br>T-shirt (W) | |
| U–V<br>United States (n)<br>U.S. (a)<br>upside-down (a)<br>vice president<br>vice versa (W) | W<br>workstation | X–Y–Z<br>x-axis<br>x-ray (v) (W)<br>X-ray (n) (W)<br>year-round<br>zeros (W-preferred spelling)<br>zip code | |

## SAMPLE DOCUMENT STYLE SHEET

| Bibliography Style | Footnote Style |
|---|---|
| Christos, Lois. _International Law Regarding Water Rights_. Delta, Utah: Waddingham Press, 1998.<br><br>Sullivan, John, and R. Hull. "Coaching College Hockey" in _Hockey Week_, Nov. 1996. | ✡ Statistics based on 1990 National Survey. |

General Notes on Typography

italicize foreign words not in Webster's

caption style:
Figure 1-1   Capitalize first word only; no period at end of caption
Headings:
1st level: boldface, all caps
2nd level: upper and lowercase (initially cap all important words:   One in a Million)
3rd level: initially cap first word only

Miscellaneous Notes

widows (less than three-quarters of a line at the top of a page) and orphans (four or fewer letters on a line unless the letters are a word) are unacceptable.

## House Style Sheet

Some companies you proofread for may give you a *house* style sheet, which would be used in combination with the document style sheet. A house style sheet includes issues that an organization might want handled consistently in all documents they produce. For example, your company (that's you if you are "the house") might prefer to always spell out numbers zero through ninety-nine, except in measurements; as in two programs, but 2 bytes or 2 miles.

Here is a portion of a sample house style sheet:

### Pacific Advertising Agency

accents: not with capital letters (entrée, but ENTREE)
don't use series commas
comic strip and radio program titles: in quotes
magazine and record album titles: ital

airdate
a.m.
catalog
disc (compact disc, disc jockey)
disk (computer disk)
Northern California
point-of-sale advertising (POS)
PR firm
SASE (an SASE)

## Client Style Sheet

As the name implies, decisions that are specific to a certain client go on a client style sheet. These are particularly helpful if you are proofreading for several clients. For example, a client might require that the company name always appear on one line, never carrying part of it to the next line, as does Hewlett-Packard. (Have you ever noticed that Hewlett-Packard in text is always hyphenated, but in their logo where Hewlett is on one line and

Packard is directly below it, it is *not* hyphenated?) Or a client might prefer a term used a particular way. Aloha Medical prefers **medium size hospital**, as opposed to **medium-size hospital** or **medium-sized hospital**. The client style sheet tells you what to do for Aloha Medical.

Since you might have clients in the same or similar fields, the client style sheet helps avoid confusion. Using the above example, Aloha Medical prefers **medium size hospital**, but St. Cloud Pediatric Center prefers **medium-size hospital**. It is sometimes hard to remember who prefers what, but with the client style sheet, you don't have to try to remember or find someone who does, or go look for the answer in a project you did earlier for the client. You save yourself time and energy by simply looking at your client style sheet.

Here are examples of partial client style sheets for clients of Pacific Advertising Agency:

### Casey Travel Consultants

use series commas
brochure titles: ital

airfare
A.M.
carry-on luggage
dos and don'ts
sightseeing

### Maxie Records

song titles: in quotes
years: the sixties, the 1960s, and '60s

air date
audiotape
CDs
lip sync (n.)
lip-synching (v.)
Top 40

---

**INSIDER TIP**

If a client's style choice differs from your house style, the client's preference usually prevails. When this happens, make a note on the client style sheet that this is "contrary to house style." Again, this saves time. When someone sees something on the client style sheet that they know differs from house style, they don't have to find out which style prevails. That decision has already been made.

---

## Other Style Sheet Tips

No matter how many style choices were made before the project came to you, new issues will always emerge. Depending on such concerns as the size of the project or who is responsible for making style decisions, there are a few different ways to handle unexpected issues that arise during the proofreading stage.

If decisions are up to you, as soon as an issue comes up that is not on the style sheet, decide how you want to handle it and add that to the style sheet. If someone else has to decide, try to get an answer before you continue your project.

Another option for handling questionable items is to query them. "Flag" anything in question (with clips, sticky tags, or anything handy). Then, when a decision is made, you can add the preferred form to the style sheet and easily find all other occurrences of the issue because they are marked with your helpful tags.

---

**INSIDER TIP**

IMPORTANT! Never assume anything and never assume you do not need to check or change something because you are "pretty sure" someone else will. When in doubt, check it or tag it for you or someone else to check later. Take the time to be sure and to be thorough.

---

---

**INSIDER TIP**

In long projects, you may want to take an additional step when recording something on the style sheet: Record the page number on which you made your style choice. Using the "prohibition" example again, if on page 6 of your document you see it as lowercase and decide that is how it should be throughout the project, record this on your style sheet and write "page 6" next to it. Then on page 22, you see *Prohibition* used in the same context. You change the *P* to lowercase because that is the decision you made. As you continue through the project, it appears that 90 percent of the time *Prohibition* appears initially capped. So you change your mind and decide it should appear initially capped throughout. Now it is easy to go back and find where you need to change the word to initially capped—it is on page 6. You can also find where you changed it anywhere else in the project after page 6, from your marks. Remember, if you do change your mind, change the style sheet.

---

## Decisions, Decisions

The person responsible for making style decisions varies from organization to organization.

When you are the only one involved in the process, it is usually easier (unless you are the kind to examine every decision to the nth degree). Of course, always start with established rules and conventions. That means, when you have what you consider a problem situation, take the time to find out if someone has already made the decision for you, like the always invaluable *Webster's*. No need to reinvent the wheel.

Sometimes decision making is as easy as following the general style of the project, as in the previous "prohibition" example.

Other times, you need to follow house style or industry standards. At times, your focus needs to be on saving time and money by making the fewest changes. With no other guidelines, you might make a decision simply because that is the way you like it done. As long as you are consistent, that works too.

---

**INSIDER TIP**

**When in doubt, go with the way the word appears most—but be consistent.**

---

There will be times, of course, when you are not the one to make a style decision. But if *you're* not, *someone* is going to have to. So, when you come to something that is inconsistent or unclear, query it! Put a tag on the page in question and if you can, call someone and get the answer right away. Some publishers also ask that you indicate the page number in the original manuscript it came from. If you can't get an answer, or if you have an issue that cannot be resolved right away, circle the issue in question in the text and write your question in the margin or on a sticky tag. As soon as a decision is made (by you or your client), add it to the style sheet. It is important that you ask the question or make your comment so it is clearly understood.

---

**INSIDER TIP**

**When you query or make comments, be polite, precise, and concise, and you can't go wrong.**

---

## Late Changes

Often decisions are not made until the middle of a project, or after you have already proofed it. A change at this time may affect several parts of the project, not just one. Consider, for example, a name change to the title of a book chapter or newsletter article that was **"Computer-aided Design"** to **"Computer-Aided Design"**—initially capping the *A* after the hyphen. This would affect the table of contents and might also affect other hyphenated titles, since you want the style to be consistent. It might affect running heads (chapter titles at the top of each page in books). And it might have to be changed in the body of the text if used there. You get the idea. So, think carefully before you make or suggest a midstream style change. But if it needs to be done, take the time to consider everywhere that the text might be affected, and then make all the necessary changes.

## CROSS-REFERENCES

In the text you are working on, *cross-references* are references to other parts of the book or project—such as another page or chapter, a figure, a graph, or a table. When you come to a cross-reference, circle it in the text and make a notation in the margin. (In publishing we usually use "xref .") Before the reference is checked:

Then when the reference has been verified, put a small check mark above your notation in the margin. This tells everyone that it has been verified and does not need to be checked again.

In almost any document, page numbers may change frequently, chapters may be moved around or their titles changed, graphs deleted, and so forth. When this happens, cross-references may need to be reverified. If they are marked, they are at least easy to find.

It is also important to verify that figures and graphs contain the information cited in the text. For example, if the text says, "See the two different computer configurations in Figure 1-1," make sure that there is, in fact, a Figure 1-1; that it does contain two computer configurations; and that the two are, indeed, different. Or, if it says, "You can see in the graph above that the population increased in 1997," you need to be sure that the graph accurately displays this information, and that the graph is, indeed, "above" (not on a previous page, which sometimes happens as things get moved around). In this last example, if the information in the graph does not match the text, and you are proofreading someone else's material, you need to query the text *and* the graph, since you may not know which one needs to be changed.

# Chapter 3

## The Basics Made More Basic

This chapter focuses on the specific areas noted earlier that you should pay attention to while proofreading: correct spelling, grammar, punctuation, and sense, always considering consistency. It also addresses some of the problem situations that seem to arise most often.

### SPELLING

#### Typos

Typos are usually the easiest errors to spot since they *look wrong*. As you read carefully, they leap out at you:

> *In response to your las letter* . . .

Since there is no such word as **las**, it is very noticeable. However, in a line that says

> *The people need to pay attention or the won't understand* . . .

you might overlook the missing *y* on **the** because **the** is a word.

As you read, you often anticipate what is coming next, and tend to read in phrases. That won't work in proofreading. You must read each word individually.

At the same time, as in the preceding "the/they" example, you need to be sure the writing makes sense. As you sharpen your skills, the ability to catch typos becomes second nature.

---

**INSIDER TIP**

**PAY PARTICULR ATTENTION TO ITEMS IN LARGE TYPE. You probably saw this one—PARTICULR instead of PARTICULAR—but most people tend to just glance at large type instead of reading it carefully. Now you won't make that mistake.**

---

## Misspellings

Misspelled words can be the hardest errors to catch. Generally a word is misspelled because it looked right to the writer.

How do you know if a word is misspelled? The best way to improve spelling is to read a lot in your spare time, because words begin to look right. Here is a handy rule to use in the meantime: If as you are proofreading (and pleasure reading) any word causes you to hesitate and wonder if it is spelled correctly, even for a second, you need to look it up. At the end of this book is a list of commonly misspelled words that you can consult to save time.

A good dictionary is vital. Although there are several excellent ones, the accepted standard reference in the publishing field is *Webster's Collegiate Dictionary, Tenth Edition*. This is the only one I use for *all* my clients. Does it matter which one you use? Sometimes. Styles change throughout time. For example, in an earlier *Webster's* edition, the word **life-style** was hyphenated. Now it is one word—no hyphen. Some other dictionaries still show it as hyphenated. When you are striving for consistency, sticking with one dictionary provides a consistent model to follow.

---

**INSIDER TIP**

When you come to a word with a questionable spelling, don't stop right then to look it up. Put a tag on it and keep reading. That way you don't break your train of thought. This is also a good idea when checking questionable word divisions at the end of lines of text. When you have finished your first readthrough you can do all the dictionary work at once. This is an efficient technique that also gives you a break from the close work of proofreading.

---

## Word Divisions

Proofreading includes making sure *word divisions*—where a word is divided (or breaks) at the end of a line—are made correctly. You would be surprised how often words (according to our "word bible"—*Webster's*) do not break where you think they should. Even when you sound out a word and think you are sure of the syllables, unless you are *absolutely* sure, you need to look it up:

> *In both the school and business worlds compu-*
> *ters have become a necessity. But basic know-*
> *ledge cannot be replaced—we still need to know*
> *what to ask and how to get the answers.*

The correct divisions of these words are

**com-put-ers**
**knowl-edge**

Also, some words break differently depending on their meaning. Here is one example:

**pro-ject**       *to plan for the future*
**proj-ect**       *a specific job*

As mentioned previously, just put a tag on each question-able break as you proofread. When you are through with the first readthrough, you can look them all up at once. It is much easier, faster, and more efficient this way.

---

**INSIDER TIP**

**Put a sticky tag on the inside cover of your dictionary with a list of words you come across often, but can never seem to remember how they should break. (The word *sec-ond* was on the inside cover of my dictionary for two years before it finally found a permanent home in my mind's memory bank.)**

---

I hear someone out there saying, "But my computer checks spelling *and* word breaks." Well, your daily newspaper provides ample evidence that computers really "miss the mark" when it comes to ensuring correct spelling and word breaks. Jay Leno shows off some of his favorite newspaper goofs in a segment each week on *The Tonight Show*. Newspapers are right about 80 percent of the time, but you want 100 percent accuracy. You and your dictionary know the difference even if your computer doesn't.

## GRAMMAR

Reading for grammar is more difficult than reading for typos and spelling errors. Grammatical errors are not as obvious, and the text does not look as blatantly wrong. Some common problems, however, can be corrected rather easily once you know what to look for. Again, grammar checking programs can be a real help, but they do not cover everything. In addition, they are very time-consuming, and not everyone has one of these programs.

## Wrong Words

Many wrong words are obvious; however, those that sound similar but have different meanings give a lot of people trouble. **Affect** and **effect** are good examples.

> **Affect** is a verb and means to influence:

> *His good looks did not **affect** me at all, but his sense of humor did.*

> **Effect**, on the other hand, is usually used as a noun, and is a result:

> *His sense of humor had a positive **effect** on our relationship.*

Two words that are confused more often than any others are **that** and **which**. Use **that** to introduce a clause that is essential to the meaning of the sentence. Use **which** to introduce a clause that is not essential. In the latter instance, **which** is always preceded by a comma.

> *I have a job **that** is very fulfilling, **which** is important to me.*

When **which** is used to refer to something, it doesn't take a comma.

> *Think carefully about **which** word to use.*

On pages 78–80 there is a list of words that are often confused. Once you know which words might be a problem, you will be able to look them up and make sure they are used correctly.

---

**INSIDER TIP**

If you are having trouble learning the correct usage of a pair of words you tend to confuse, teach yourself in which situation to use *one* of the words. Then in all other cases, use the alternate word. For example, use *insure* when referring to physical safety or insurance. Use *ensure* in all other instances.

---

## Agreement

Another particularly troublesome area for many people is *agreement*. A good grammar handbook can be a big help, but here are some things that may be of instant help.

When a sentence starts out talking about *you*, it shouldn't switch to *I* or *we*.

Agreement also means number agreement. When the subject is singular, you need a verb that "agrees" with the subject:

> **One** of the computers **is** down.
>
> **There's a** movie I really want to see.

If you have a plural subject, the verb must also be plural:

> The **computers** in the main library **are** down.
>
> **There are lots** of movies I really want to see.

There is also agreement in time. If you begin talking about things happening now, you need to continue in the present:

> I **run** every day, then **take** a shower and **eat** breakfast.

However, if you have finished one thing, you need to have finished the other:

> *I **ran** every day, then **took** a shower and **ate** breakfast.*

When you get "out of time" in your writing, you really lose your reader.

> *I **run** every day, then **took** a shower and **eat** breakfast.*

Like spelling, knowing correct agreement gets easier as you become accustomed to looking for it.

## Compound Words

Deciding when to use a hyphen to form a compound word can be complex. Your best reference, as always, is a current dictionary. (Remember the "life-style/lifestyle" example from earlier?) When a term is not in the dictionary, use your own judgment about whether to hyphenate or not. Ask yourself, "Will the term be confusing without the hyphen?" For example, in

> *a short hemmed skirt*

is the **skirt** short (better written as a short, hemmed skirt), or is the **hem** short (a short-hemmed skirt)? The reader should not have to guess what you mean. Hyphens can be very helpful in making your meaning clear.

*The Chicago Manual of Style* has an excellent guide for the hyphenation of compound words.

---

**INSIDER TIP**

When a compound modifier contains an adverb that ends in -ly, the two words are *never* hyphenated:

**highly motivated**

---

## PUNCTUATION

Following are five common punctuation problems. They are so common, you will probably see at least one of these in almost every project you proofread.

### Commas

Aside from some established rules, use of commas is a matter of judgment and choice. Use commas to indicate a brief pause in thought, as you would if you were speaking. And use them to avoid confusion.

In a series of items, do you use a comma before the word **and**?

> *red, green, and blue*

> or

> *red, green and blue*

For years, the rule was to use the serial (or *series*) comma before the **and**. It is no longer a rule; now it is a style choice. Either usage is correct; just be sure the choice is consistent throughout the project. Even if you have chosen not to use the serial comma, if you have a sentence in which the meaning would be confusing without the final comma, use it.

### Colons

A colon is most often used to add the meaning "as follows" without saying it in words.

> *This book will be helpful to a variety of people: students, desktop publishers, and professional proofreaders, to name a few.*

In a sentence, initially cap the first word after a colon when it begins a complete sentence.

> *Creating documents on-screen is still a lot of work: Computers only do what we tell them to do.*

One other note about colon usage: Do not use a colon immediately after a verb.

> *An employer most often looks for these qualities: honesty, integrity, and dedication.*

but

> *The qualities most employers look for are honesty, integrity, and dedication.*

## Punctuation with Quotation Marks

There are a few exceptions (as there always seem to be in this unique language of ours), but as a rule, commas and periods go inside quotation marks; semicolons and colons go outside.

For exclamation points and question marks, it depends on whether the punctuation refers to the material within the quotation marks or not:

> *At some point in a child's life, a parent asks, "When did you learn that?"*

but

> *Do you agree with the saying "All's well that ends well"?*

---

**INSIDER TIP**

One obvious (but often missed) necessity is that quotation marks travel in pairs (as do parentheses). When you see an opening or closing quotation mark (or parenthesis), *doublecheck* to see that you also have its mate—and that it is in the right place.

---

## Periods Inside or Outside of the Closing Parenthesis?

Believe it or not, this is an easy one. If the enclosed material is a complete and independent sentence, the period belongs inside:

> *Hockey players have to be able to skate as well as they walk. (Their safety may depend on it.)*

When the enclosed material is part of the sentence, the period belongs outside:

> *My son plays hockey outside in the dead of winter (even at 20 degrees below zero).*

---

**INSIDER TIP**

Use only one space after terminal punctuation—a period, question mark, or exclamation point. For a long time the rule was to use two spaces, but no more. Really!

---

## Apostrophes

Apostrophes seem to give many people problems, but the rules are relatively simple. They are used mainly in two instances: for contractions and to show possession.

In contractions, add an apostrophe where you leave out the letter or letters:

*do not = don't*

*let us = let's*

*could have = could've*

*I would = I'd*

To show possession, use the rule: For words both singular and plural that do not end in *s,* add an apostrophe *s.*

*Jean's koala, the men's bats, the people's agreement*

Often the apostrophe tells us whether the thing owned belongs to one or more people. In **the girls' coats,** we have several girls, each owning one or more coats. In **the girl's coats,** however, we have only one girl who owns more than one coat.

Authorities differ on the rule for words that already end in *s.* Some say that you add an apostrophe *s* to everything. Others say that for words that already end in *s,* add only an apostrophe. For example:

*Charles' snake*

or

*the Jones' party*

The house style or the client style may determine which rule to use.

---

**INSIDER TIP**

**Punctuation following an italicized word is *italicized!* Punctuation following a boldfaced word is *not* (see "coats" in the paragraph above), except when the whole sentence or design element is boldfaced (as in the "Warning!" example for boldface markings on the Proofreader's Marks Plus Examples on page 10).**

---

Four word pairs that give the most trouble are the WITY*
(pronounced witty) words:

| Contraction | | Possession |
| :---: | :---: | :---: |
| who's | W | whose |
| it's | I | its |
| they're | T | their |
| you're | Y | your |

*Courtesy of Dr. Ann Longknife.

Notice that it is always the contraction that takes the
apostrophe. Possessive pronouns (such as its, his, hers, theirs, and
yours) never do.

# Chapter 4

## What Comes Next?

Now that you have read the text of the project looking for proper grammar, punctuation, spelling, consistency, and sense, what comes next?

Stage 1, the first readthrough, was covered in Chapter 2. Now we'll discuss the next seven stages. For each stage, go through the entire manuscript (referred to as a *pass* through the manuscript) to check the particular item you are focusing on. It sounds like it will take forever to do this, and you may feel you do not have the time. But it is *worth* the time, and it won't take as long as you think. In fact, to complete these last stages of a 500-page book, it might only take a few hours.

If you are proofreading for a publisher, you may receive a set of *sample pages*. These give examples of how each *design element* in a book should look. Following is a list of the design elements usually shown in sample pages, and an excerpt from a set of sample pages.

- Chapter Number (CN)
- Chapter Title (CT)
- Level 1 Heading (1)
- Level 2 Heading (2)
- Level 3 Heading (3)
- Numbered List (NL)
- Bulleted List (BL)
- Figure Caption (FC)
- Table Caption (TC)
- Running Head or Running Foot (RH or RF)
- Page Number (Folio)

# Chapter 8

# Résumé Writing

## Form and Substance

Akmdfh nfjks ksais oksldj kdk sksl nks. Bjhd kdj cksjjinsjhs jsj-sisiuej,nnjsdhyuei. Jk idndklz ksus yuei iewn kjsjk jslaj djjs; skkal llksjhsd. Akmdfh nfjks ksais oksldj kdk sksl nks. Bjhd kdj cksjjinsjhs jsjsisiuej,nnjsdhyuei. Jk idndklz ksus yuei iewn kjsjk jslaj djjs; skkal llksjhsd.

## Tailor Your Résumé to Each Prospective Employer

Akmdfh nfjks ksais oksldj kdk sksl nks. Bjhd kdj cksjjinsjhs jsj-sisiuej,nnjsdhyuei. Jk idndklz ksus yuei iewn kjsjk jslaj djjs; skkal llksjhsd. Akmdfh nfjks ksais oksldj kdk sksl nks. Bjhd kdj cksjjinsjhs jsjsisiuej,nnjsdhyuei. Jk idndklz ksus yuei iewn kjsjk jslaj djjs; skkal llksjhsd.Akmdfh nfjks ksais oksldj kdk sksl nks.

**Figure 11-1 The Logical Screen for Dungeon.**

Kk idndklz ksus yuei iewn kjsjk jslaj djjs; skkal llksjhsd. Akmdfh nfjks ksais oksldj kdk sksl nks. Bjhd kdj cksjjinsjhs jsj-sisiuej,nnjsdhyuei. Jk idndklz ksus yuei iewn kjsjk jslaj djjs; skkal llksjhsd.

Table 1-1 Icap, no punctuation

| Column One | Column Two |
|---|---|
| xxx | yyy |
| aaa | bbb |
| ooo | sss |

Akmdfh nfjks ksais oksldj kdk sksl nks. Bjhd kdj cksjjinsjhs jsjsisiuej,nnjsdhyuei. Jk idndklz ksus yuei iewn kjsjk jslaj djjs; skkal llksjhsd. Akmdfh nfjks ksais oksldj kdk sksl nks. Bjhd kdj cksjjinsjhs jsjsisiuej,nnjsdhyuei. Jk idndklz ksus yuei iewn kjsjk jslaj djjs; skkal llksjhsd.Akmdfh nfjks ksais oksldj kdk sksl nks.

1. Akmdfh nfjks ksais oksldj
2. kdk sksl nks. Bjhd kdj cksjjinsjhs jsjsisiuej,nnjsdhyuei sksl nks. Bjhd kdj cksjjinsjhs jsjsisiuej,nnjsdhyuei

3. Jk idndklz ksus yuei iewn
4. kjsjk jslaj djjs; skkal llksjhsd

Akmdfh nfjks ksais oksldj kdk sksl nks. Bjhd kdj cksjjinsjhs jsjsisiuej,nnjsdhyuei. Jk idndklz ksus yuei iewn kjsjk jslaj djjs; skkal llksjhsd. Akmdfh nfjks ksais oksldj kdk sksl nks. Bjhd kdj cksjjinsjhs jsjsisiuej,nnjsdhyuei. Jk idndklz ksus yuei iewn kjsjk jslaj djjs; skkal llksjhsd.Akmdfh nfjks ksais oksldj kdk sksl nks.

- Akmdfh nfjks ksais oksldj
- kdk sksl nks. Bjhd kdj cksjjinsjhs jsjsisiuej,nnjsdhyuei sksl nks. Bjhd kdj cksjjinsjhs jsjsisiuej,nnjsdhyuei
- Jk idndklz ksus yuei iewn
- kjsjk jslaj djjs; skkal llksjhsd

Akmdfh nfjks ksais oksldj kdk sksl nks. Bjhd kdj cksjjinsjhs jsjsisiuej,nnjsdhyuei. Jk idndklz ksus yuei iewn kjsjk jslaj djjs; skkal llksjhsd. Akmdfh nfjks ksais oksldj kdk sksl nks. Bjhd kdj cksjjinsjhs.

It is the responsibility of the author, copy editor, or book designer to determine what these elements should look like. It is the proofreader's job, however, to verify that they all appear correctly. Remember that we are here to help achieve a quality end product. Sometimes that means finding things that those before us missed—as those after us may find things we have missed. But let me reiterate, if you find **errors**, correct them; if you see **areas for improvement**, query them, don't change them.

---

**INSIDER TIP**

**If you find you are changing the same thing more than twice—for example, all page numbers are a consistent style, but they do not match the sample pages—STOP! Call your client to see if perhaps the style was changed, but just not recorded on the style sheet or sample pages.**

---

The previous list of design elements actually serves as a good partial outline for the following discussion of the next seven stages of proofreading.

## STAGE 2: CHAPTER NUMBER AND CHAPTER TITLE

You can check these in the same *pass* (pass through the manuscript). Look to see that all the chapter numbers and chapter titles of each chapter look the same. What exactly are you looking for? Same *T*ypeface (how the type appears; for example, roman or italic? Palatino or Gothic?), same *S*ize, and same *P*lacement on the page (TSP). You'll hear about the TSP trio quite a bit in this book. Also, reread the chapter titles for any typos. (Remember the earlier Insider Tip about proofreading large type?)

## STAGE 3: HEADINGS

*Headings* are the titles used to introduce sections of a chapter, article, and so on. Headings in a book often have different levels of importance. In publishing, these levels are designated as A, B, C, and so on, or 1, 2, 3, and so on. Different level headings each look different. Level 1 headings may have all capital letters, for example. Level 2 headings may be upper/ lowercase (abbreviated u/lc). *Upper/lowercase* means that most words in the title are initially capped. The exceptions are prepositions, conjunctions, and articles of four letters or less. The lowercasing of these elements of speech is a standard *style*, but not a rule. So if your client prefers lowercasing those articles of three letters or less or icapping all words in headings, that is fine—as long as all instances are handled consistently.

---

**INSIDER TIP**

**In a heading, initially cap all words following a colon or an em dash (—), and all first and last words in a heading, even prepositions, conjunctions, and articles. For example:**

*Cooking: The Art of It*

*The Meal Is Ready—And So Are We*

*Finally, Dessert to Finish Up*

---

Style varies when it comes to capitalization within a hyphenated word: **Self-Employed** or **Self-employed**? Once again, if no style is set, and all occurrences are handled consistently, then either is correct.

An example of a level 1 heading appears at the top of this page, "Stage 3: Headings." An example of a level 2 heading appears in this book on page 50, "Numbered Lists."

In this stage, check to see that all headings of the same level look the same: typeface, size, and placement on the page (flush left aligned with the text, as are the headings in this book, or with a paragraph indent?).

## STAGE 4: NUMBERED LISTS AND BULLETED LISTS

Numbered lists and bulleted lists can be checked in one pass.

### Numbered Lists

In numbered lists you want to look for five things.

1. First, are the numbers in each list in correct consecutive order, with no numbers skipped?

2. Is the TSP trio consistent? Is the spacing after the number but before the text consistent (as it certainly is on this page)?

3. Is the text right justified (text set with all lines even at the right margin), as it is in this numbered list? Or is it ragged right (text set with lines forming an irregular right margin), as in the example on page 52?

4. Do the second and third lines of each numbered item align under the number or under the text in the first line?

5. Is there an equal amount of space between each numbered item, as well as above and below the numbered list?

```
┌─────────────────────────────────────────────┐
│              ■ INSIDER TIP ■                  │
│  When you have a numbered list of ten or more items, │
│  the numbers should align over the last digit: │
│                                               │
│     9. Budget Rent a Car                      │
│    10. Del Monte Foods                        │
└─────────────────────────────────────────────┘
```

## Bulleted Lists

In bulleted lists, check for all the same things, except for consecutive numbering, of course. But do check to see that bullets are consistent. Bullets can range from simple round dots ( • ) to elaborate symbols ( ❧ ). Make sure they are all the same size and shape.

## STAGE 5: CAPTIONS

There are different kinds of captions, three of which are most often used. An *art* caption is an unnumbered title of a piece of art, as in a picture or graph. For example:

> *Child at play*

A *figure* caption is a numbered title of a piece of art:

> *Figure 1-1 Expected U.S. population growth 1996–2000*

A *table* caption, or title, describes the material in a table (a table shows columns of information, as below):

**Table 1-1 Price List.**

| Item | Description | Price |
|------|-------------|-------|
| 91475 | Fax machine | $499.95 |
| 122854 | Calculator | $ 38.99 |

---

**INSIDER TIP**

Numbered figures and tables are traditionally *called out* in text, meaning that there is a reference to the numbered item in the text, such as, "see Figure 3-3." These numbered figures and tables should appear as close as possible to where they are called out in text. The art should not precede the callout, and it should not appear more than three pages after the callout.

---

For such a small bit of text as a caption, there is a surprising amount you need to pay attention to. The obvious things you already know—typeface, size, and placement in relation to the art or table. Let's use our figure and table captions from page 51 as examples and see what else there is to watch out for. Are the following elements used consistently?

| | |
|---|---|
| *Figure* | • *Is this word icapped or all caps?* |
| *1-1* | • *Is a period or a hyphen used between the numbers?* |
| | • *Does punctuation (period or colon) follow the numbers?* |
| *Caption text* | • *Is the spacing consistent between the number and the text?* |
| | • *Is only the first word icapped, as in the Figure 1-1 example; or upper/lowercase (handled as a heading in terms of capitalization), as in the Table 1-1 caption?* |
| *Price List.* | • *Is a period used at the end of the caption? (No in Figure 1-1; yes in Table 1-1.) Punctuation is often handled consistently, regardless of whether the caption is a complete sentence or a sentence fragment.* |

---

**INSIDER TIP**

If there are numbered figures and tables, write the words *Figures* and *Tables* on a piece of paper. While you proofread, make a hashmark each time you come to one of these numbered items. This tells you, at a glance, where you are in the numbering.

Figures ⊞

Tables |||

---

While you are checking table captions, look at the information contained in the table, too. Are all column headings handled consistently with regard to typeface, size, and placement?

In this case, placement applies to headings and columns of information. The headings may be centered over the column of information:

| Age | Street Address |
|:---:|:---:|
| 9 | 909 Seacliff Avenue |
| 5 | 818 Aptos Way |

Or flush left (aligned with the first item in the column of information):

| Name |
|:---|
| Alexa |
| Sam |

---

**INSIDER TIP**

When a table begins on a left-hand page and continues to a right-hand page (called *facing* pages), column headings are not usually repeated. If a table goes from a right-hand to a left-hand page (called a new *spread*), column headings usually are repeated. Also, if the table continues on a new spread, sometimes the caption is repeated, adding the word *continued* after it. It is a style choice whether to include this *continued* line, but it is probably easier for the reader if you do.

---

## STAGE 6: RUNNING HEADS AND FOLIOS

*Running heads* are the headings at the tops of pages (*running feet* are at the bottoms of pages) that tell the reader what he or she is reading. In publishing, often the running head on the left-hand (*verso*) page is the book title and the running head on the right-hand (*recto*) page is the chapter title:

*36   Go Ahead...Proof It!*

*What Comes Next?   37*

In a school paper or newsletter, for example, running heads are often the same on both pages.

*Folio* is another word for page number. Even-numbered page numbers appear on the left-hand pages; odd-numbered page numbers appear on the right-hand pages. As in the previous example, running heads and folios on the left-hand page are usually flush left, and on the right-hand page are flush right.

Unless the chapter running heads change throughout the book (if they match each section of a chapter, for example), you can check running heads and page numbers at the same time. As always, check these elements for the TSP trio. Also, check that the sequential page numbering is correct.

## STAGE 7: TABLE OF CONTENTS

Here, you need to verify that the table of contents is a correct reflection of the material it references. A book table of contents usually includes titles and page numbers for the introduction; chapter titles; level 1, 2, and sometimes level 3 headings; bibliography; and index. A newsletter may list the titles and page numbers of the articles that appear inside.

Go through the book pages to verify that the wording of the chapter or heading titles in the table of contents exactly matches the titles in the text. If the title of a chapter is

> *Step One: Skiing the Bunny Slope*

the table of contents should not show any of these:

> *Step 1: Skiing the Bunny Slope*
>
> *Step One—Skiing the Bunny Slope*
>
> *Skiing the Bunny Slope*

You need to check every page against the table of contents, verifying that titles and page numbers are correct and that none were left out. Then take a look at the table of contents on its own to see that all the elements (numbers, spacing, style, and so on) are consistent.

## STAGE 8: A FINAL LOOK

You are almost done. Now, take another few minutes to give the project one final visual appraisal. Go through it page by page to see how the material *looks*. Are there any areas of blank space that look bad? Is spacing between headings and text equal? Are there any really short lines of text that you did not notice before? Overall, is it pleasing to the eye?

---

**INSIDER TIP**

**If you can avoid it, don't proofread when you are tired. Sometimes you have to. Maybe your term paper is due tomorrow. Or maybe your client *has* to have the job done by 9:00 a.m. tomorrow, and at 10:00 p.m., you still have 50 pages to go. Pace yourself and take a break of at least 10 minutes every half hour to an hour. Even though your quitting time will be later, you will double your efficiency.**

---

If you have taken the time to go through all eight stages, you have performed an excellent quality proofread. At this point, you have completed your proofread of the *first proofs* of the project. Your job as a proofreader may be done. Now the project goes back to a desktop person (maybe you) to input the changes you have marked.

## FINALS CHECK

But who checks to see that all the changes were made correctly? In publishing, someone always proofreads the *second proofs*. This check is sometimes called a *finals check*. Sometimes the project comes back to you for second proofs, and sometimes it is done *in-house* (by the client's staff). Whether you are working for someone else or yourself, this is an important step. Even if you are working on a small project and there are not many changes, you would be surprised how many things can go wrong in the input stage. As a rule, this check will not take very long.

---

**INSIDER TIP**

The average time for proofreading first proofs is 10 pages per hour; for second proofs it is 20 pages per hour.

---

Follow these steps for a thorough finals check:

1. Check that all changes from previous page proofs were made correctly and that no new errors were introduced. Do this by checking the change itself, as well as reading the text immediately above, below, and to the left and right of it.

2. Check that no copy was dropped (accidentally omitted). This is especially important when copy has been moved around. The best way to do this is to check the first and last words of each line. If they do not match, something has changed. You need to find out what and if it was changed correctly. (As an alternative, you can check the first and last words of a paragraph while visually scanning the lines in between.)

3. If headings or page numbers have changed, reverify that the table of contents is correct.

4. If chapter titles or page numbers have changed, recheck the running heads (or feet) and page numbers.

If you have the time, do a straight read (reading the final version without comparing it to the manuscript) one more time. This is particularly advisable if several people have worked on the project. It gives you a very objective view of the material. You've been so intent on looking for so many things, stepping back and reading the material as if you were the audience can be very beneficial.

# Chapter 5

## Special Circumstances

Every proofreading project is different in terms of the level of proofreading you or your client requires. Following are some helpful hints to be aware of when working in a few specific fields. These suggestions are recommended **in addition to** what has already been discussed.

### PROOFREADING FOR A PUBLISHER

Working for a publisher can be more complex than you might find with other clients, because there may be more elements of a project a publisher wants you to pay attention to. At the same time, it can be much simpler, and this applies to both book and periodical publishers. Because there may be several proofreaders working on the project—all looking for errors in the text—unless you are the first proofreader, there are often fewer errors by the time the material comes to you; therefore, there is less for you to catch.

Each time you make a change, in addition to marking changes in the margin, mark each change in one of two ways. If the change is because the page proof did not match the manuscript, write *pe* (for printer's error; the printer or typesetter is responsible for the expense of this change) next to your marking in the margin. If you, as the proofreader, initiate the change, then write *ea* (for editorial alteration; the publisher is responsible for the expense of these changes) next to your marking in the margin.

Most publishers have a house style sheet (discussed on page 26), and for books, each project will have a document style sheet (see example on pages 22–25) provided by the author and editors. When you have queries, you will most likely have one contact who, if unsure of the answer, will make it his or her business to find out. Also, most publishers will supply you with a complete set of sample pages (see sample on pages 46–47). The more information you have, and the more attention paid to the project before it is handed to you, the easier your job should be.

## Nonfiction

Even if you do not have familiarity with a technical subject matter, you can still do an excellent proofreading job. Just follow the stages discussed earlier, take your time, and you'll do fine. As you read you will develop a feel for the material. When something you are reading is beyond the scope of your technical knowledge, you have to trust that the author and editors are comfortable with the way the material is presented. But just like any other project, if some wording really confuses you, go ahead and query it—it might also confuse the audience.

---

**INSIDER TIP**

**Doublecheck acronyms, for example, What You See Is What You Get (WYSWYG). Oops, left out a letter. It should be WYSIWYG. Acronyms are usually pulled from words in a name that are icapped—Family and Medical Leave Act (FMLA).**

---

In nonfiction, you often have an increased number of special elements (graphs, tables, figures, and so on). So there are more instances in which you need to check that the references in the text correctly relate to these elements (see Cross-References on page 31).

*Computer-Related Material*

The most difficult part of proofreading books about computers and computer programming is grasping an understanding of the usage of computer-specific terms. It is a slower read when, instead of English words, you are reading about the std.lbio string, or the AcquireView function. Here again, you rely on the authors' and editors' knowledge and, hopefully, a thorough style sheet. In addition to words, numbers, punctuation, and design styles, the style sheet needs to include a list of type conventions for computer-specific terms. Here are just a few examples of what might appear on a computer manual style sheet:

- double-click
- hot-key control
- list box
- scroll bar
- toolbar
- wildcard

**Type Conventions**
- Buttons—icaps, no quotes: Cancel button
- Classes—all caps: STATUSCLASSNAME
- Functions—u/lc, closed up, followed by parens: ChooseColor()
- Parameters—ital, caps where shown: *lpszText*

Computer books sometimes have sections or lists of computer *code* (programming language for the reader/user). This code is usually set in a completely different typeface from the regular text—maybe OCRB:

```
XPosition :=0; //These fields are not used//
```

Sometimes these lists of code are called *listings* and have a numbered caption. Be sure to find out if your client wants you to review this code. If the answer is yes, you most likely will not need to understand the code, but you do need to check closely to

---

**INSIDER TIP**

Most of the terms listed on page 61 will not be on a style sheet. (The style sheet would be book length.) If you are curious about, say, the spelling, capitalization, or hyphenation of a word or phrase, look at the computer code (see page 61) the material discusses. Your answer will often be there. Also, many figures are *screen captures* (pictures of what appears on the computer screen being discussed), and may offer some help. For example, if the text says to click on the *Ok* button, there may be a picture of that button in the screen capture, so you can see if *Ok* is correct, or if it should be *OK*.

---

make sure no lines of code have been dropped going from manuscript to first proofs or from first proofs to second proofs.

Sometimes these listings are several pages long. When they continue to a new spread, captions are not usually repeated (as they are with tables). However, many publishers add a *continued line*—maybe **continued on next page** at the bottom of the right-hand page, and **continued from previous page** at the top of the left-hand page. If this is a house style, pay close attention to the use of these lines. In books, text often gets added, deleted, or moved around, and these continued lines can end up where they don't belong.

## Fiction Books

There are two things to pay particular attention to in fiction books: character names and time sequence. Again, it is the authors' and editors' responsibility to make sure these are correct, but . . .

You will probably get a list from the publisher of characters' names: spellings of their full names, any pet or nicknames, and sometimes their relationship to a few of the other characters. An example might be

> *James Ray Johnson (Jim; called Ray by his*
> *family; husband of Dorothy)*

If you do not get this list, it is helpful to make one as you go.

Time sequence is actually a little easier. As you read, jot down on a piece of paper when in time the story begins—Monday, 10/8, or summer 1953, for example. Or just make a mental note of the time of day. As the hours, days, years, whatever, tick by in the story, make a note of it. You might not need this information, but it never hurts to be prepared.

For example, the text says

> *Barbara finished her breakfast, bundled up in*
> *her coat and scarf, and rushed out the door for*
> *her conference.*

But earlier text (and your chronological list) shows that it is July in the story, (so would she be bundling up in her coat?) and it is 5:00 P.M. (so she would not be finishing her breakfast). Something is wrong, so query these inconsistencies.

## ADVERTISING COPY

Here, more than anywhere else, you need to take your cue from your client. Always ask if there is a house style guide. Some might have a short word list; others may have extensive ones. (Hewlett-Packard's style guide is 236 pages long.) If they do not have a guide, make sure you keep your own client style sheet. Many grammar, punctuation, and even spelling rules are cast aside in advertising. It seems the term *editorial license* was created by this field. Remember the old ad slogan:

> *"Treats Your Wood Good"*

Grammatically, of course, it should have been "Treats Your Wood Well," but that would not have been as catchy.

Another example:

*Hang it on a mantle. Over a door. Anywhere.*

Accept that established rules do not always apply in advertising. Be restrained with what grammar and punctuation changes you make, and use your judgment on what to query. Experience in the field, and with each client, will give you a better feel for what is acceptable and what is not.

---

**INSIDER TIP**

**This applies to all jobs! Don't be frustrated if a client does not make changes you have indicated—even when you are *sure* you are right. It is the proofreader's job to mark errors, but the client's choice and responsibility to accept or reject the changes marked, for whatever reason—style choices, time constraints, and so on.**

---

## RETAIL CATALOGS

Publishers of retail catalogs usually have style guides that cover not only words and numbers, but also special elements. Some of these might include:

- Price
- Special or Sale Price
- Measurements
- Fractions
- Additional Charges (like Shipping & Handling)
- Return Policies
- Ordering Information
- Delivery Information
- SKUs (ordering item numbers)
- Keys (letters designating a pictured item and the corresponding description)

Proofreading catalogs is usually pretty straightforward—not a lot of queries or problems. But the special elements listed above are critical, so it is important that you take your time and proofread in stages, constantly paying attention to the TSP trio.

Following is an abbreviated sample page from a retail catalog.

On each page, start by verifying that the keys on the art match the titled descriptions. Next, read everything on the page. Finally, look at the special elements to see that they are styled consistently and follow the client guidelines. That's it!

**A** Warm, wide, wonderfully dramatic. These **Gold-Plated Frames** add a decorative touch to your favorite photographs. Display horizontally or vertically; wall mount or tabletop.
**Large Frame** (shown right), 8" x 10"
#28-1523  $27.00
**Medium Frame** (shown far right),

Measurements ———————— 5" x 7"
#28-1525  $18.00
**Small Frame** (not shown)

Fraction ——————— 3 1/2" x 5"
#28-1527  Regularly $10.00 ——— Price

Sale Price   **Special Price  $9.00**

A

Key

**B** Sit back, relax, and enjoy a steamy cup of your favorite brew. These entrancing **Carmela Coffee Cups and Saucers** are creamy white Italian pottery. Imported.
*Set of 4*
#28-1535  $25.00

B

SKU

*Our Guarantee: If for any reason you are not satisfied with your purchase, please return the item. We will gladly replace merchandise or issue a refund.*

### The TCQ Gift Box, With Our Compliments

Upon request, we'll send your selection in our elegant gift box—free of charge. Not available for items marked ◇.

16 • T C Q  H O L I D A Y  B A Z A A R

# Chapter 6

## After You're Filled In

Okay, now you know what you are looking for. Following are a few proofreading warm-up exercises. The corrected versions appear on pages 69–70.

On pages 71–72 is the big challenge: your "final exam." Proofread once again the PDU Campus News newsletter that was shown in Chapter 1 and see how much more you are aware of. When you are finished, compare this version to the one you did in Chapter 1.

Next, compare your proofread version to the corrected one on pages 73–74. Since sticky tags would have been a little awkward to include on every copy of this book, queries are listed using the numbering system discussed in Chapter 1: a number next to each item in question, with the corresponding query on pages 75–76. The queries are worded as they might be on a sticky tag, precise and concise.

Because there will always be some issues that are judgment calls on the part of the proofreader about what to change and what to query, you may not have marked or queried all the same items as on the corrected version.

In reviewing the corrected version, even if you do not agree with a change or query, consider why it might have been marked. Seeing what someone else has done may make you aware of something to pay attention to in the future. Remember,

*Learning to proofread is an ongoing process. Each time a new situation or question presents itself is an opportunity to learn something new!*

## Fiction

"Where did Butch go"? Joe asked. Jenny should have known that pesky monkey wouldn't sit still. Suddenly, Jenny heard Joe laughing. "Come see this." Joe called. I turned the corner into the kitchen to see Butch up on the counter—doing the dishes! Well, maybe he wasnt so pesky afterall.

## Press Release

### New Business Offers Extra Help

Shirley Guys firm provides assistance for those who work with words. Onsite or offsite, do you need proofreading, copy editing, indexing? We can furnish efficient professionals that can take care of your editoral needs.

## Minutes

The meeting was called to order this morning at 10:30 a.m. All our members were present. After the reading of the minutes, Bill Brown, Chairmen of Finance, reported   need for additional funds to cover costs incured by the clean-up campaign your club sponsored.

## CORRECTED VERSIONS OF FICTION, PRESS RELEASE, AND MINUTES PROOFREADING EXERCISES

### Fiction

"Where did Butch go?" Joe asked. Jenny should have known that pesky monkey wouldn't sit still. Suddenly, Jenny heard Joe laughing. "Come see this," Joe called. I turned the corner into the kitchen to see Butch up on the counter—doing the dishes! Well, maybe he wasn't so pesky afterall.

## Press Release

### New Business Offers Extra Help

Shirley Guys firm provides assistance for ℣

those who work with words. Onsite or off-

site, do you need proofreading, copy edit- ⓒⓤ

ing, indexing? We can furnish efficient

professionals that can take care of your who

editoral needs.

## Minutes

The meeting was called to order this

morning at 10:30 a.m. All our members

were present. After the reading of the

minutes, Bill Brown, Chairman of a

Finance, reported need for additional the

funds to cover costs incured by the r

clean-up campaign your club sponsored.

# PDU CAMPUS NEWS

VOLUME 10, NUMBER 8          FALL ISSUE

## The Tide is Turning—Gray

*By Ann Longknife*

I entered my new literture class expecting the usual eager (and not so eager) young students who would grow wise from my relayed wisdom. I was surprised, however, to see an old lady sitting in the front row. She was Betty, 86 years old, in school becuase she wanted to know more about literture. Betty is only one of the older students now coming to college. They are changing the classroom, generaly for the better.

In the past, the older student was an anomoly in the community college classroom, but that has changed. Re-entry women return to learn new skills. Some people who have lost their jobs return for retraining. And many return to enhance their lives now that they are established and their children are grown.

These students weren't considered valuble by the State of California. A few years ago Governor Wilson decreed, and the legislature agreed, to raise fees, from $13 a credit hour to $50, for those students who already have a degree. Enrollment dropped and the schools collected neither the $13 nor the $50. Last year the law was rescinded—now the older students are back.

There varied experiences give a new perspective to class discussions so the younger students learn about many different views rather than just their own or the instructors. In turn, the older students learn how young people think which gives them better rapport with their own children and, often, their colleagues at work.

The instructor, however, needs to make this sharing a positive experience. I've found some ways to do this. I call every one by their first name, which makes the students feel they are equals. Sometimes, older students monopolize the conversations. This can be deadly, so I call on people by name. That way everyone gets to contribute. When I share papers with the class, I make sure I acheive a balance between those of older students and younger. Most importantly, I treat the answers of all the students with respect. If I favored one group, the class would not work.

The baby boomers, as we've been told repeatedly, are older—and perhaps wiser, for they are coming back to learn what they missed earlier. They can be a source of income for the community college, but, more importantly, they can promote a lively, energetic environment where all students, regardless of age, can get a better education.

## By my Own Rules: Confessions of a freelance writer

*By Michelle Goodman*

Self-employed, innovator, entreprenuer, consultant, freelancer, independent contractor, jill-of-all-trades, small business owner, armchair professional, artist, creative type, dreamer. Chances are you know somebody you'd classify as one of these. Between my accountant and my family, I've personally been called as everything from "1099 worker" to "slacker".

As a self-employed writer, I'm often regarded as rule-breaking rebel, a curiosity in a world of synchronized commuting and coffee breaks. And justifiably so. Take my obscure work habits, for instance: While you're rushing off to the office at 8:15 a.m. in your dry-cleaned suit, I'm propped up

*Continued on page 3*

**1**

*Continued from page 2*

in bed, wearing a ratty old bathrobe, pecking away at my laptop computer. When Letterman's over and you turn off the light to sleep, I'm nursing a pot of coffee, trying to wring a few more productive hours out of the day. Tomorrow during your 3 o' clock meeting I might be napping in the park, hiking along the beach, or watching Oprah.

When you work for yourself, you're not just breaking the pre-existing rules of the 9-to-5 workforce, you're writing your own comandments of employment, then rewriting them as you go. I can e-mail press releases and advertising copy I write to a handful of clients I'll probably never even meet face to face, thanks to my faithful computer modem. And sometimes I'll work 15-hour days for a straight week, then send out my invoice and kick back and relax the following week.

People always ask me how I can work in my house, alone all day long, tempted by all the procrastination-inducing distractions of home (fridge, TV, phone, newspaper). Then they want to know what on Earth could have compelled me to give up the steady paycheck and benefits package that I may or may nod be blessed with were I a "regular" company employee. For me the how and why of my choice to work this way is one and the same: Being master of my own destiny—free to stay up late and sleep in, saved from the stress and exhaustion of the dreaded 5-day-a-week commute, free to spend more time doing what I want to do—is far more rewarding than the so-called advantages of any "real" job.

## A Profile of ESL Students At PDU

As social, economic, and political circumstances create the conditions for immigration to the U.S., a large number of speakers of other languages are striving to become literate in English. In recent years, PDU has experienced considerable growth in the number of language minority students seeking to become literate in English.

Figure 1 depicts students' ESL proficiency in terms of their current course level (i.e., 841, 842,

843 and 844): 39.7% of student are enrolled in 844-level coursework; 29.6% in 843-level; 14.7% in 842-level, and 15.1% in 841-level.

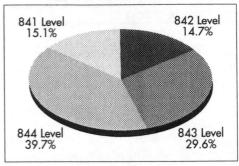

**Figure 1**
Current ESL Proficiency Level

Figure 2 shows that between approximately one-quarter to one third of students expressed an interest in taking ESL courses during each of the four following times:

1. 7:00 am–8:00 am M–F (29.3%)

2. Saturday mornings (26.8%)

3  5:00 pm–6:00 pm M–F (20.4%)

An additional 25.6% indicated "other times; these included Sunday mornings, Sunday evenings, Saturday evenings, and 6:00am M-F courses.

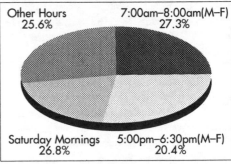

**FIGURE 2**
Interest in alternative days for ESL classes

2

# PDU CAMPUS NEWS

VOLUME 10, NUMBER 8                                          FALL ISSUE

## The Tide is Turning—Gray

*By Ann Longknife*

I entered my new literature class expecting the usual eager (and not so eager) young students who would grow wise from my relayed wisdom. I was surprised, however, to see an old lady sitting in the front row. She was Betty, 86 years old, in school because she wanted to know more about literature. Betty is only one of the older students now coming to college. They are changing the classroom, generally for the better.

In the past, the older student was an anomaly in the community college classroom, but that has changed. Reentry women return to learn new skills. Some people who have lost their jobs return for retraining. And many return to enhance their lives now that they are established and their children are grown.

These students weren't considered valuable by the State of California. A few years ago Governor Wilson decreed, and the legislature agreed, to raise fees, from $13 a credit hour to $50, for those students who already have a degree. Enrollment dropped and the schools collected neither the $13 nor the $50. Last year the law was rescinded—now the older students are back.

There varied experiences give a new perspective to class discussions, so the younger students learn about many different views rather than just their own or the instructors. In turn, the older students learn how young people think which gives them better rapport with their own children and, often, their colleagues at work.

The instructor, however, needs to make this sharing a positive experience. I've found some ways to do this. I call every one by their first name, which makes the students feel they are equals. Sometimes, older students monopolize the conversations. This can be deadly, so I call on people by name. That way everyone gets to contribute. When I share papers with the class, I make sure I achieve a balance between those of older students and younger. Most importantly, I treat the answers of all the students with respect. If I favored one group, the class would not work.

The baby boomers, as we've been told repeatedly, are older and perhaps wiser, for they are coming back to learn what they missed earlier. They can be a source of income for the community college, but, more importantly, they can promote a lively, energetic environment where all students, regardless of age, can get a better education.

## By my Own Rules: Confessions of a freelance writer

*By Michelle Goodman*

Self-employed, innovator, entrepreneur, consultant, freelancer, independent contractor, jill-of-all-trades, small business owner, armchair professional, artist, creative type, dreamer. Chances are you know somebody you'd classify as one of these. Between my accountant and my family, I've personally been called everything from "1099 worker" to "slacker."

As a self-employed writer, I'm often regarded as a rule-breaking rebel, a curiosity in a world of synchronized commuting and coffee breaks. And justifiably so. Take my obscure work habits, for instance: While you're rushing off to the office at 8:15 a.m. in your dry-cleaned suit, I'm propped up

Continued on page 2

1

73

1 *Continued from page 2*

in bed, wearing a ratty old bathrobe, pecking away at my laptop computer. When Letterman's over and you turn off the light to sleep, I'm nursing a pot of coffee, trying to wring a few more productive hours out of the day. Tomorrow, during your 3 o'clock meeting, I might be napping in the park, hiking along the beach, or watching Oprah.

When you work for yourself, you're not just breaking the pre-existing rules of the 9-to-5 workforce, you're writing your own commandments of employment, then rewriting them as you go. I can e-mail press releases and advertising copy I write to a handful of clients I'll probably never even meet face to face, thanks to my faithful computer modem. And sometimes I'll work 15-hour days for a straight week, then send out my invoice and kick back and relax the following week.

People always ask me how I can work in my house, alone all day long, tempted by all the procrastination-inducing distractions of home (fridge, TV, phone, newspaper). Then they want to know what on earth could have compelled me to give up the steady paycheck and benefits package that I may or may not be blessed with were I a "regular" company employee. For me the how and why of my choice to work this way is one and the same: Being master of my own destiny—free to stay up late and sleep in, saved from the stress and exhaustion of the dreaded 5-day-a-week commute, free to spend more time doing what I want to do—is far more rewarding than the so-called advantages of any "real" job.

## A Profile of ESL Students At PDU

As social, economic, and political circumstances create the conditions for immigration to the U.S., a large number of speakers of other languages are striving to become literate in English. In recent years, PDU has experienced considerable growth in the number of language minority students seeking to become literate in English.

Figure 1 depicts students' ESL proficiency in terms of their current course level (i.e., 841, 842,

843, and 844): 39.7% of students are enrolled in 844-level coursework; 29.6% in 843-level; 14.7% in 842-level; and 15.1% in 841-level.

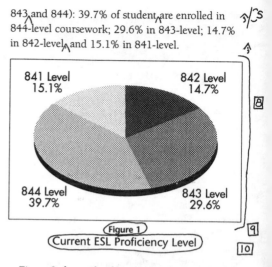

841 Level 15.1%
842 Level 14.7%
844 Level 39.7%
843 Level 29.6%

**Figure 1**
**Current ESL Proficiency Level**

Figure 2 shows that between approximately one-quarter to one third of students expressed an interest in taking ESL courses during each of the four three following times:

1. 7:00 am–8:00 am M–F (27.3%)
2. Saturday mornings (26.8%)
3. 5:00 pm–6:00 pm M–F (20.4%)

An additional 25.6% indicated other times; these included Sunday mornings, Sunday evenings, Saturday evenings and 6:00 am M–F courses.

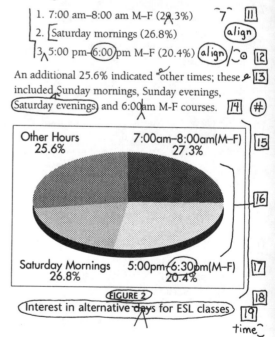

Other Hours 25.6%
7:00am–8:00am(M–F) 27.3%
Saturday Mornings 26.8%
5:00pm–6:30pm(M–F) 20.4%

**FIGURE 2**
**Interest in alternative days for ESL classes**

time

2

## PDU CAMPUS NEWS
## CORRECTED VERSION QUERIES

1. Change to students?

2. Okay to begin sentence with a conjunction?

3. Cap?

4. Instructors' or instructor's?

5. Bottom-align columns?

6. Stet, or no periods, as on p2?

7. Okay to begin sentence with conjunction?

8. Amounts add up only to 99.1%. Change amounts to equal 100%?

9. Stet, or change to all caps to match Figure 2?

10. Stet, or change to icap only to match Figure 2?

11. Changed to match Figure 2 below, okay? 29.3% would bring percentage total to 102.1%; 27.3% means the total is 100.1%.

12. Stet, or 6:30 to match Figure 2 below?

13. Okay to delete quotation marks; or add close quotation marks? If adding, then after *other,* or after *times?* How about deleting quotation marks and changing text to Other Hours, to match Figure 2?

**14.** Move up, to follow chronological order?

**15.** Amounts add up to 100.1%. Okay?

**16.** Sizes of pie slices don't seem correct; e.g., slice for 20.4% is larger than that for 26.8%. Are percentages or slices wrong?

**17.** Stet, or 6:00 as in numbered list item 3 above?

**18.** Stet, or change to icap only to match Figure 1?

**19.** Stet, or change to upper/lowercase to match Figure 1?

# Appendix A

## Words Often Misspelled

accommodate
accumulate
acknowledgment
allotment
all right
analyze
annihilate
benefit
bouillon
caffeine
colonel
conscientious
counterfeit
discipline
embarrass
entrepreneur
envelope
existence
familiar
fiery
fluorescent
foreign
harass
height
hemorrhage

innuendo
inoculate
judgment
liaison
lightning
likelihood
liquefy
maintenance
maneuver
necessary
niece
occasion
occurrence
parallel
paraphernalia
personnel
pneumonia
precede
prejudice
privilege
proceed
process
questionnaire
realtor
receive

recommend
restaurant
rhythm
ridiculous
separate
siege
silhouette
skeptical
sophomore
spaghetti
succeed
supersede
surprise
surveillance
synonymous
thorough
tranquillity
unanimous
usage
vacuum
veterinarian
waiver
weird
withheld
yield

# Words Often Confused

| | |
|---|---|
| **accept** | To receive willingly |
| **except** | To exclude |
| **advice** | Suggestion or counsel |
| **advise** | A verb meaning to give advice |
| **affect** | A verb meaning to influence |
| **effect** | A result |
| **all ready** | Prepared |
| **already** | Previously |
| **anxious** | To anticipate with uneasiness |
| **eager** | To anticipate with enthusiasm |
| **awhile** | "Wait awhile." |
| **a while** | "Wait for a while." |
| **choose** | To pick |
| **chose** | Already picked |
| **cite** | To quote |
| **site** | Location |
| **complement** | Something that completes, or makes perfect |
| **compliment** | Praise |
| **conscience** | Sense of moral goodness |
| **conscious** | Aware |

| | |
|---|---|
| **ensure** | To make certain |
| **insure** | To obtain insurance; to guarantee protection or safety |
| **everyday** | One word when used as an adjective |
| **every day** | Each day |
| **farther** | At a greater distance |
| **further** | In addition to |
| **its** | Belonging to *it* |
| **it's** | Contraction of *it is* |
| **later** | Afterward |
| **latter** | The second of two things |
| **lay** | To place or put down |
| **lie** | To recline |
| **lets** | Allows |
| **let's** | Contraction of *let us* |
| **loose** | Not tight |
| **lose** | Opposite of win |
| **passed** | A verb—past tense of *pass* |
| **past** | Use when it is not a verb |
| **principal** | Main |
| **principle** | Rule |
| **stationary** | Not moving |
| **stationery** | Paper |
| **than** | Compares |
| **then** | Subsequent action |

| | |
|---|---|
| **their** | Possessive of *they* |
| **there** | In that place |
| **they're** | Contraction of *they are* |
| | |
| **to** | Toward |
| **too** | Also |
| | |
| **who's** | Contraction of *who is* or *who has* |
| **whose** | Shows ownership |

# Appendix B

## Glossary of Publishing-Related Terms

**aa**   (Stands for *author's alteration*.) A change made by the author in the page proof stage. Author's alterations, or some part of them, may be charged against an author's royalties.

**ascender**   The part of a lowercase letter that extends above the body of the letter, as in the letters *d, f, k,* and *t.*

**back matter**   Material that follows the main body of the text, such as an appendix, glossary, or index.

**bad break**   When the text is produced in its final form, any unsightly arrangement of type; for example, a heading appearing as the last line on a page, a paragraph ending with just one or two letters on a line, or only one or two words at the top of a page.

**baseline**   The line on which the bottoms of all letters sit.

**blind folio**   A page number that is counted but is not printed on the page. (This often occurs on the first page of a chapter.)

**blueline**   Photographic prints prepared from the text or art for offset reproduction. This is the last copy before the book goes to press.

**boldface**  Type that is thicker and darker than the rest of the text with which it appears.

**camera-ready copy**  Typewritten material, art, and so on that is ready to be photographed for reproduction without any further changes.

**caps**  Capital letters.

**caption**  The title of a picture, table, illustration, and so on.

**caret**  A symbol used to indicate that an insertion to text is to be made.

**character**  A number, letter, punctuation mark, or any other symbol.

**condensed type**  Characters that are narrower than normal.

**copy**  Material to be used in producing a printed work.

**copyediting**  Correcting and preparing a manuscript for typesetting.

**copyright**  A protection granted by law that gives the holder exclusive right to make or have made copies of the copyrighted material.

**crop**  To trim portions of a photograph or illustration to a desired size.

**cross-reference**  A reference made in one part of the material to a different portion (chapter, page, and so on) of the material.

**dead copy**  Manuscript that has been typeset and all corrections made, so it is no longer needed.

**delete** To eliminate.

**descender** The part of a lowercase letter that extends below the body of the letter, as in *g*, *j*, and *q*.

**ea** (Stands for *editorial alteration*.) When proofreading, this mark should accompany changes that the proofreader or editor initiates, instead of a correction made because the page proof does not match the manuscript; for example, correcting the spelling of a word that was accidentally misspelled in the manuscript and missed by the copy editor.

**ellipsis** Three periods (or dots) used to indicated an intentional omission.

**em** A unit of measure equal to the space occupied by the letter *M*; usually used in *em dash* or *em space*.

**en** A unit of measure equal to the space occupied by the letter *N*; usually used in *en dash* or *en space*.

**flush left** (or **flush right**) Copy set along a left (or right) margin.

**folio** A page number.

**font** A complete assortment of type of one size and typeface, including caps, lowercase letters, punctuation, and so on.

**footnote** A note appearing at the bottom of a page that refers to information given somewhere on that page.

**front matter** Material that precedes the main body of the text, such as a title page, copyright page, dedication, acknowledgments, table of contents, preface.

**glossy**  A photograph with the glossy finish preferred for reproduction work.

**gutter**  The inner margins of facing pages (where a book is
bound), or the blank space between columns of type.

**hair space**  A very narrow space used to separate letters or numbers that are too tight.

**hanging indent**  Text that is set with the first line of a paragraph
flush left and the lines following it are indented.

**initial cap**  The first letter of a word is capitalized.

**italic**  A slanted variation of a typeface.

**justify**  To set text so that all lines are even at both right and left
margins.

**kern**  To adjust awkward or unsightly spacing between letters or
words.

**layout**  The order in which the book or material is presented.
Also, the design of the book, such as size of the book, size of the
type page, typeface, and so on.

**leaders**  Dots or dashes used to guide the eye across the page, as
in a table of contents.

**leading** (or **line space**)  The space between lines.

**letter spacing**  Inserting spaces between the letters of a word to
expand it.

**ligature**  Two or more connected letters, such as *fi*.

**lightface**  The ordinary roman or italic print, not boldface.

**lowercase**  Letters not capitalized.

**margins**  Blanks areas that border the typeset page.

**measure**  The width of a full line or column to be typeset.

**orphan**  A fraction of a word appearing alone on a line, or a fraction of a line appearing alone at the top or bottom of a page.

**pe**  (Stands for *printer's error*.) Anything shown correctly in the manuscript that the printer or typesetter set incorrectly.

**pica**  A printer's unit of measure equal to about 1/6 of an inch or 12 points, often used in measuring line lengths.

**point**  A printer's unit of measure equal to 1/72 of an inch.

**press run** (or **print run**)  In publishing, the number of copies that are to be printed.

**proofreader's marks**  Standardized symbols used to indicate corrections to be made to copy.

**query**  A question.

**ragged right** (or **ragged left**)  Copy set with uneven right (or left) margins.

**recto pages**  Right-hand (odd-numbered) pages. (Chapters often begin on a recto page.)

**river**  (Also called *river of white*.) A streak of white space caused by spaces between words in several lines. A river of white can run vertically or diagonally.

**roman**   Type that is straight up and down, as opposed to slanted italic type.

**rule**   Straight, decorative, thin, thick lines used for several purposes, such as borders, boxes, or separating items.

**running head** (or **running foot**)   The title at the top (or bottom) of each page. This could be the author's name or the book, chapter, section, or school subject title, for example.

**sample pages**   A set of pages giving examples of how design elements in a book should be set.

**sans serif**   Perfectly plain letters with lines of uniform thickness, and without serifs.

**serif**   Short strokes that extend from the main strokes of a character. (This book is in a serif typeface.)

**small caps**   Capital letters smaller than the standard capital letters of a particular font.

**spine**   The part of a book binding connecting the front and back covers.

**stet**   A term that indicates material marked for correction should be restored to its original form (before the correction was marked).

**subscript**   A small number, letter, or symbol printed partly below and to the side of another type character.

**superscript**   A small number, letter, or symbol printed partly above and to the side of another type character.

**transpose**   To switch the positions of two letters, words, sentences, paragraphs, and so on.

**trim size**   The final size of a whole page, including all margins.

**type (text) page**   The area of a page that contains all the printed matter, running heads (or feet), and page numbers.

**typeface**   The full range of type—letters, numbers, punctuation, and so on—of the same design.

**typographical error**   An error made by the typesetter. Affectionately known as a *typo*.

**uppercase**   Capital letters.

**verso pages**   Left-hand (even-numbered) pages.

**watermark**   Name of a maker of paper produced so that the design shows when the paper is held up to the light.

**white space**   Any space on a page that does not have printed material on it.

**widow**   A short line of text alone at the top of a page.

**x-height**   A dimension equal to the height of the lowercase letters, such as the *x*, excluding ascenders and descenders.

# Recommended References

Bromberg, Murray, and Julius Liebb. *The English You Need to Know*. New York: Barron's Educational Series, Inc., 1987.

*The Chicago Manual of Style*. 14th ed., rev. Chicago: University of Chicago Press, 1993.

Glazier, T. F. *The Least You Should Know About English Writing Skills*. Form B, 15th ed. New York: Harcourt Brace College Publishers, 1994.

Griffith, Benjamin W. *Pocket Guide to Correct Spelling*. 2nd ed. New York: Barron's Educational Series, Inc., 1990.

Hooper, Vincent F., Cedric Gale, Ronald C. Foote, and Benjamin W. Griffith. *Pocket Guide to Correct Grammar*. 2nd ed. New York: Barron's Educational Series, Inc., 1990.

*Merriam Webster's Collegiate Dictionary*. 10th ed. Springfield, MA: Merriam-Webster, Inc., 1993.

Obrecht, Fred. *Minimum Essentials of English*. New York: Barron's Educational Series, Inc., 1993.

Strunk, W. J., and E. B. White. *The Elements of Style*. 3rd ed. New York: Macmillan Publishing, 1979.

Temple, Michael. *Pocket Guide to Correct English*. 2nd ed. New York: Barron's Educational Series, Inc., 1990.

Venolia, Jan. *Rewrite Right!* Berkeley, CA: Ten Speed Press, 1987.

*Words into Type*. 3rd ed., rev. Englewood Cliffs, NJ: Prentice-Hall, Inc., 1974.

# Index

advertising copy, 63–66
author, 2, 13, 48, 60–61

callouts, figures/tables, 52
capitalization, 19, 49, 52, 60
captions, 45, 51–52, 61–62
catalogs, retail, 64–66
chapter number/title, 45, 48
clients, nonpublisher, 4–5, 63–66
clients, publishers, 59–63
column headings, 53–54
comment format, 30
comparison proofreading, 16–18
computer books, 61–62
computer tools, 1, 15, 36
consistency, 3–4, 18–20, 30, 33–35,
    40, 49, 50, 52
continued lines, 54, 62
copy editor, 2–3, 14, 19–20, 48
cross-references, 31–32, 60, 82

design elements, 45–48, 64–66
dictionary, 18–20, 29, 34–36, 39, 88
dropped copy, 57

ea (editorial alteration), 59, 83
editorial license, 63
editorial proofread, 4
editors, 2, 13–14, 60–61. *See also* copy
    editor
exercises, 7–9, 67–76

facing pages, 54
fiction books, 62–63
figures, 31–32, 45, 51–53, 60
finals check, 56–57
flag (query), 28, 30
folio (page number), 45, 54–55, 57,
    81, 83

glossary, 81–87
grammar, 1, 36–39, 63–64, 78–80

grammar/spell check, computer, 1,
    15, 36
graphs, 31–32, 60

hard copy, 15
headings, 45, 49–50, 53–54
hyphenation, 3, 19, 34, 39, 49

icapped (initially capped), 19, 49, 52,
    60
in-house work, 56
Insider Tips
    acronyms, 60
    assumptions, 28
    callouts, figures/tables, 52
    changes not made, 64
    changes, repeated, 48
    compound words, 39
    computer terms, 62
    consistency, 3, 30
    extra check, 17
    figure numbers, 53
    heading capitalization, 49
    house/client style, 28
    large type, 34
    list alignment, 51
    online proofreading, 15
    pages per hour, 57
    physical considerations, 16, 56
    punctuation, 42–43
    query/comment format, 30
    read out loud, 19
    spelling checks, 35
    style sheet, page number, 29
    table numbers, 53
    tables, 54
    thoroughness, 28
    word breaks, 36
    word usage, 38

list alignment, 51
list, bulleted, 45, 51

list, numbered, 45, 50–51
listings (code), 61–62
Longknife, Dr. Ann, 8, 44, 71, 73

manuscript, 2, 13–14, 16
memo example, 13–15, 20
misspellings, 34–35, 77
newsletter exercises, 7–9, 67, 71–76

nonfiction books, 60–61

online proofreading, 15

page number (folio), 45, 54–55, 57,
    81, 83
page proofs, 3, 16–18, 56–57
pages, sample, 45, 60, 86
pass, 45
pe (printer's error), 59, 85
physical considerations, 16, 56
placement (TSP trio), 48, 50, 52, 53,
    55, 65
possession, 42–44
proofreading
  comparison, 16–18
  computer tools for, 1, 15, 36
  defined, 1–3
  editorial, 4
  level of, 18, 59
  marks, 4–5, 10–11, 18, 85
  online, 15
  references. See reference books
  stages, 4, 16, 45–48
    1: first readthrough, 18
    2: chapter number/title, 48
    3: headings, 49–50
    4: lists, 50–51
    5: captions, 51–54
    6: running heads/folios, 54–55
    7: table of contents, 55
    8: final look, 55–56
  straight read, 16–18, 57
publishers, 2–3, 59–63
publishing terms, 2–3, 81–87
punctuation, 1, 40–44, 52, 63–64

query, 3, 16, 18, 28, 30, 48, 60, 67

readthrough, 18
reference books
  *Chicago Manual of Style, The*, 18, 39,
      88
  list of, 88
  *Webster's Collegiate Dictionary*, 18–20,
      29, 34–35, 88
running foot, 45, 54–55, 57, 86
running head, 45, 54–55, 57, 86

sample pages, 45, 60, 86
size (TSP trio), 48, 50, 52, 53, 55,
    65
spell/grammar check, computer, 1,
    15, 36
spelling, 33–36, 63–64, 77
spread, 54, 62
stages of proofreading. *See* proofreading stages
style sheets, 3
  client style sheet, 26–28, 63
  computer books, 61–62
  document style sheet, 21–25, 60
  house style sheet, 26, 28, 30, 60, 63,
      64
  industry standards, 20, 30
  late changes, 30–31
  page number, 29
  style choices, 18–21, 28–30

table of contents, 55, 57
tables, 31–32, 45, 51–54, 60
tags, query, 28, 30
tags, spelling check, 35–36
technical books, 60–62
tips. *See* Insider Tips
typeface (TSP trio), 48, 50, 52, 53,
    55, 65
typographical errors (typos), 15,
    33–34, 87

verb agreement, 38–39

*Webster's Collegiate Dictionary*, 18–20,
    29, 34–35, 88
WITY words, 44
word divisions, 35–36